The Rational
CHRISTIAN FAITH

A Step-by-Step Guide into the Faith
That Is Anything but Blind

JEFF McCONNELL

To the Lord of lights. May my life be a harmonious note in the symphony of Your will.

For all the souls that read this book, may the God of truth, grace, and peace enlighten you toward His gospel.

To my beloved wife, who patiently endured the long hours associated with this book, and to my children, who will inherit these thoughts when I'm gone.

Table of Contents

The Rational
CHRISTIAN FAITH

Introduction

Every worldview I chose, it seemed, edged me toward belief.
MARTHA BECK

Every person on this planet possesses a worldview. A worldview is a set of *traditional, philosophical and/or religious perspectives by which you view the world.* Some elements of our worldview accurately assess the world that we live in, some aspects are flawed, and others are relative to us as individuals and outside of the bounds of right and wrong. Nevertheless, people in all aspects of society—doctors, tradesmen, professors, scientists, teachers, politicians, even toddlers—are passively influenced by what is considered to be the "norm" in the culture they grew up in.

As soon as we are able to remember, we begin the process of interacting with the world's surrounding influences, uncritically adapting viewpoints without the proper knowledge on how to filter them. From the youngest ages, children observe the social behaviors that will kickstart the processes of conforming to the world through imitation. At some point we then add to or replace the traditional views and values that our parents raised us with and begin to explore and adopt some

of the numerous philosophical influences found in film, litera-
ture, popular theory, pop culture, and music. These mediums
plunge us deeper into the newest and most dominant views in
contemporary thought. It is early on in life that many of these
influences become cemented into our subconscious—forming
a *default worldview setting* that stays with us more or less
permanently—unless challenged.

Obviously, it would be ridiculous to assert that all default
beliefs are false or even harmful to us. It is true, however, that
all of us unknowingly hold on to numerous core beliefs (even
entire worldviews) that are illusory, false, and in desperate
need of discarding. It is an ethical obligation to rid ourselves of
error through the examination of the views that we hold dear
and possess a readiness to surrender these views if truth calls
from another direction. We must possess the willingness to
comb through the compost heaps of cultural error in order to
find the nugget(s) of truth hidden within. The inner desire for
truth must trump over any contentment with personal illusions.

As we investigate the question of worldviews, let us begin by
acknowledging that the most truthful worldview ought to have
some basic elements before being accepted. Firstly, *the worldview ought to be reasonably sound*—nonsense in reason is
nonsense in reality. This means that the worldview must make
clear and reasonable assumptions about the world by making
logical sense, without violating sensible thought or foundational laws of logic, such as the law of non-contradiction.

The second condition is that *the worldview must be consistent with basic experience*. A worldview is an attempt to bring
the diversities of human experience in areas like science, justice, love, mathematics, sexual desire, religiousness, and curi-
osity into a whole working and understandable system. This
does not mean that we need to be able to explain absolutely

everything, but that everything will make some sense in the framework of the worldview. Worldviews that are unable to explain the basics like consciousness or justice deny basic tenants of human experience and can't be a proper worldview.

Lastly, I would argue that the worldview defended *must be practically livable* if it were to be true. I should be able to live out a belief system consistently; if not, it is worthy of no further consideration. A worldview should seek to explain why the world and universe are the way they are—attempting to explain how we *already* live and why we *already* view things the way we do. Why are things the way that they are and how ought we to live is a part of the whole worldview mission.

For instance, let's imagine that a certain religion existed that held the view that every type of plant and creature is considered to be a "person" equal to that of a human. In other words, John Smith is a person with as much worth and value as a sea sponge—they are equals. As a result of this understanding, this religion's goal seeks to create worldwide morally-binding laws in every country, where all forms of plants and animal life are protected from being harmed in any way, including eaten or cut apart for consumption.

To logically follow this worldview would ultimately lead to the death of all humans on Earth, since we need to eat other forms of life in order to survive. But this is a contradicting goal at its root, because human life too is valuable. It seems that if you enforce these laws, you kill off all humans, and if you don't enforce these laws, then inevitably something must die and become food for humans to eat. This would be problematic for our original main doctrine.

The problem is we seem to already know that there is a hierarchical value assigned to living things on an individual level. Any life form that possesses personal attributes such as self-awareness or intelligence seems to obviously possess more worth and value. The clover has less value than an ant, an ant has less value than a mouse, a mouse has less value than a dolphin, etc. The human is therefore of a much higher worth than the mosquito. If a choice came down to a person putting either one human or one mosquito to death, it is obvious which choice would be the moral one.

A worldview that cannot discern the common-sense morals of human worth compared to a plant and is ethically unrealistic can hardly be a viable worldview option. This worldview then fails all of the criteria above. It is not reasonably sound since we have the moral knowledge that a difference of value exists in living things; it is therefore also not consistent with our base experience, and its moral implications are practically unlivable and unthinkable. This religion is worthy of being discounted, since it fails to explain many obvious things that we experience.

The best worldview is the one that explains reality the best. This is a basic test that all worldviews should be able to submit to in order to be considered both rational and true.

This leads us to the purpose of this book—is the worldview of Christ and His followers one seated upon a reasonable foundation or not? I argue that not only is Christianity the only rational religion based upon credible historical, forensic, and even scientific elements, but that it rationally towers the other worldviews that are expressed today—especially in foundational ethics, logic, and living consistency according to that worldview. *If the Christian faith is the truth of God, then it reasonably follows that it also carries authority in all the areas of life that it speaks to such as religion, philosophy, ethics, and practical life.*

Many assume that Christianity is like any other man-made religion, full of primitive mythologies, errors, false statements, and endless contradictions—hardly worthy of any vested interest. In a sense, I agree with the spirit of that statement. Why would anyone want to give their life over to a set of superstitious views? But the Christian lives free from irrational views and embraces the God of objective truth, as we will see.

I have heard many arguments against Christianity and, increasingly, it seems that most challenges are little more than those circulated by the skeptics of contemporary pop culture. And yet, I truly wonder how many of those skeptics of the Christian faith have truly investigated this worldview on its own merit? Are they basing their opinion off the one-time conversation that they had with a street preacher or religious family member? How many have humbly sought out the answers to their arguments through reading capable defenders of the Christian faith, such as theologians, scientists, or apologists? How many have read the Bible for themselves to see what it says and claims about itself? I suspect not many. Wherever you might be in your journey (skeptic or not), in the following pages I hope now to bring you into a close introductory contact with some of these crucial sources and expand your knowledge on this important issue.

Two Possible Foundations

In the realm of Western worldviews, there exists a tale between two important cities of thought—the Capulets versus the Montagues, so to speak—living in animosity toward one another. Both views could be understood by asking this single question: *Why are we here and how did we get here? Do we owe our existence to natural process or a God?*

It is hard to express all of the implications hidden behind this single mega-question. Essentially, a worldview will rest on two possible foundations. The first being *if there is no God, then mankind is the standard for all things.* At this point, truth then ultimately becomes unknowable; we make our own rules, determine our own morality, and make our own destiny. We are, practically speaking, the self-appointed gods and god-desses of our world, since no higher power exists to govern or guide any of our perspectives into objective or absolute truth.

If, however, God does exist and has indeed revealed Himself to us, then it logically follows that mankind is not the standard for all things; man is instead subject to a much higher standard that already exists, and revelation must be our objective source for the truth. If God exists, then it is reasonable to assume that He has also gifted men with instinctual moral guidelines according to His law; it will be against this law that all men will be judged. To many, this is the epitome of uncomfortable thoughts and, for that reason, many tend to avoid or ignore this topic altogether.

My Presupposition

I am a follower of Jesus Christ. The Jewish Old Testament and Christian New Testament writings that make up the books of the Christian Bible unfold a colorful map with a steady com-pass for the worldview of an estimate of over 2 billion people worldwide.

After thousands of years of persecution on almost every con-tinent, and long centuries of intense skepticism by exhausted opponents, the Word of God remains the most consistent and accurate worldview in the world—it is the best-selling book worldwide for a reason. It is my goal in this book to lead every truth seeker toward an understanding of *the rational faith behind a follower of Christ.* There is only one reasonable worldview that is perfectly consistent with our natural view of the universe—allow me to introduce you to it.

Not only does God exist, but God has also announced His presence through the natural world (natural revelation) and through prophetic spokesmen of the past (special revelation) as recorded in the Bible. And yet, God's greatest manifestation was in the sending of His divine Son, Jesus Christ, who lived perfectly among us, died in anguish upon the cross for the payment of the sins of those who would come to Him, rose from the grave in a glorified resurrected state, and is now seated beside God the Father in Heaven, awaiting a return in judgment upon Earth. Jesus was God (the second member of the Trinity) in the flesh and proved this claim to deity collectively through His divinely authoritative personality, selfless works of love, unwavering service to the kingdom of Heaven, miracles, and—most importantly—the historically verified resurrection from the dead.

In a contrast to Christianity, one of the most opposed worldviews toward the Christian faith is that of atheism, which holds to the belief that there is no God. This worldview happens to be one of the most influential and dominant worldviews in Western culture today and is the view that I will challenge most in this book.

The two basic dogmatic articles of this worldview's faith system are *materialism* and *naturalism* (yes, you heard that right—atheism is indeed a faith system). It is through these philosophies that the atheist interprets and understands the world in which he lives. These two tenants of faith are their guiding assumptions for their worldview.

First, atheism is *materialistic*; this is the assumption that matter is all that there is; there is no soul, no God, no life after death, no reality other than what we can observe physically. Hence, atheists do not believe generally in any immaterial reality or spiritual dimension to the universe. Their view could be essentially summed up as "what you see is what you get."

Secondly, atheism is also *naturalistic*; this assumption says that everything can be ultimately explained through natural processes (the known or unknown laws of nature). Anything appearing to be supernatural is considered to be impossible; thus, all such supernatural claims are akin to superstitious nonsense in this view, or can be explained by a physical process that is yet to be discovered by science.

This is the predominant view of modern science, psychology, medicine, and philosophy. Due to this worldview's popularity in high academic circles and contemporary thinking, it is widely considered to be the most enlightened and rational worldview. But is this truly the case? This naturalistic and materialistic worldview that has become our culture's default worldview setting of the last few generations is ripe for some good ol' fashioned criticism.

Let the Journey Begin

With this introduction in the back of our minds, the purpose of this book is to take the reader on a journey into the Christian faith using a rational process or steps that will demonstrate that, if anything, it is the atheistic worldview that is the most irrational view, requiring far more faith to believe in than the Christian religion.

While there are numerous arguments from the natural world for God's presence throughout history, I have chosen to use the examples I thought to be the most obvious and clear for the common person. Other Christian intellectuals, philosophers, and apologists have covered these topics in more extensive detail; in fact, it is possible to find complete volumes for every argument that I will briefly touch on. However, for the purposes of this book, I have chosen to limit the scope of the arguments for those who want a broad introductory view of the rational foundations for the Christian faith. I trust this will be a valuable and convincing introductory resource.

Similarly, I would also like to say, as the 17th-century English puritan John Bunyan stated in his book *Saved by Grace*, that if you find that I am too short in these topics, this is due to my love for brevity. If you find me to be beside the truth in any of these areas, you can assign that to my fallen, ignorant, sinful nature. But if you find anything that leads you to faith in Christ and the inner desire for truth, then attribute that to the mercy of God given to both of us.

To all who will examine the natural and special revelations of God with me, it is my hope that you will find new insights and become abundantly aware that the processes of logic and reason are not foreign to Christian belief. Reason has always triumphed over any claim to blind faith. *Reason will compliment true faith, and true faith will harmonize with reason.* One cannot be sacrificed on the altar of the other, since God has clearly purposed both reason and faith for our mutual benefit.

Let us first examine the natural world to see what can be known about the fingerprint of our Creator, His attributes, and His character, and then proceed further to what is known by theologians as "special revelation," where God has revealed Himself in a far more intimate and revealing way.

Part 1

NATURAL REVELATION

1
The Knowledge of
GOD

*For the scientist who has lived by his faith in the power of reason, the story
ends like a bad dream. He has scaled the mountains of ignorance, he is about
to conquer the highest peak; as he pulls himself over the final rock, he is
greeted by a band of theologians who have been sitting there for centuries.*

ROBERT JASTROW, GOD AND THE ASTRONOMERS

*If you seek it like silver
And search for it as for hidden treasures,
Then you will understand the fear of the Lord
And find the knowledge of God.
For the Lord gives wisdom;
From his mouth come knowledge and understanding.*

PROVERBS 2:4-6

In a world rich in industrial, biological, and chemical projects, our public must rely heavily upon the mathematical precision of engineers. They are the expert minds behind numerous developments and projects that handle the very calculations that could dramatically affect the public's health and safety. The precision involved in engineering a suspension bridge, the biological factors in creating a chemically-composed cure for a disease or the discovery of a new fuel source are just a few examples to consider. If the math is mistaken on the design of the bridge, it could collapse; if the chemicals in a cure are imbalanced, then the cure may be more lethal than the disease; and if the fuel's source is too unstable, then it might be too dangerous to contain. For an engineer, accuracy with the true principles of the physical world is essential.

Isn't it strange that two people can have a conversation about the physical truths in construction, and in the next minute deny any truth when it comes to a discussion about God, the soul, or morals? It seems that in the physical categories of discussion, everyone knows truth exists, but in spiritual categories many assume that it does not, and that everyone can freely decide what is truth. Inconsistent, isn't it? This is a double standard. Here, I submit to you the introduction of another problematic worldview in our society today: *relativism, which is the denial that absolute truth exists outside of yourself (objective) and so truth depends upon personal opinion or experience within yourself or your culture (subjective).*

In today's social conversation, regarding concepts like goodness, morals, God, or spiritual reality, it is commonplace for people to embrace statements like, "There is no such thing as truth," "What is true for you isn't necessarily true for me," or my personal favorite, "To each his own."

Is it really reasonable to assume that something is what I want it to be, rather than what it actually is?

Consider for a moment what the world would be like if all truth were relative? Imagine a man with a headache searching his medicine cupboard for something to take away the pain. He finds a bottle of aspirin beside a bottle of cyanide; he reads both labels but proceeds to empty the cyanide tablets into his hand. As he brings them to his mouth, a loved one suddenly grabs his arm, saying, "Stop! Those cyanide tablets will kill you!" He responds, "Hey! Your truth is your truth, and my truth is my truth. I believe that cyanide can cure my headache. Mind your own business; to each his own."

Obviously, this man's unhinged worldview is out of touch with reality, and he is ignorant to the severity of the situation. If he continues in that belief, fatal consequences will most assuredly result.

Our culture might believe that truth is relative, but luckily no one can consistently live life in this way; otherwise, devastating scenarios like the one above would be far more commonplace. Reasoning like this is logically naïve, yet widely accepted in our culture—a culture that, interestingly enough, prides itself on being intellectually advanced.

Now, to a limited degree, certain items of personal preference may be true for one person but not for another. Taste in music or food is subjective to us, but just because some truths vary from person to person does not imply that *all* truth is relative. If God has revealed Himself to us objectively, then it follows that we must accept both God and all of His revelation as *binding upon every person* objectively. We must therefore also follow those facts of revelation to their inevitable ends, embracing even those truths we may find to be inconvenient or confusing along the way.

People do not invent truth—they discover it. It has been said that all of the mathematical formulas that we currently understand in science—the laws and constants that govern our physical universe—could be written down on a single page. Concepts of mathematics or the scientific laws of magnetism and gravity have all been in working effect before anyone had the opportunity to observe them as true. They were true before mankind existed, and they will be true after we die. Truth is true, whether we know about it or not, and so if God exists, then it logically follows that God also exists regardless of whether we personally believe it to be true or it or not.

We are also subjected to all of the physical truths that govern our Earth as well. Gravity will do its job even if you deny the existence of gravity; your blood will flow through your veins and arteries even if you deny the existence of blood flow. The spiritual world—which includes absolute morals, the consciousness of the soul, and God—behaves the same. In both places, truth behaves the same—it simply exists regardless of your personal beliefs and desires.

A blind man can deny the existence of airplanes if he wants to (since he has never personally seen one), but if he finds himself walking on an airport runway one day, what was doubted will soon become reality, and his denial of that truth will be met with very real consequences. So it is with God, if He indeed will be in the judgment seat one day.

This lack of understanding and confusion associated with the nature of truth is a deadly philosophical blind spot in our contemporary Western culture. Our lack of understanding keeps us from being open to anything existing transcendently beyond the physical world before our senses. To form a correct worldview, we must first be willing to accept that, to some degree, objective truth exists beyond all that makes up reality—both physical and non-physical. Once we understand this about the nature of truth, we are able to begin to build upon a rational worldview.

The Art of Discovering Truth

Allow me to get a bit philosophical for just a moment. Before we continue on to the topic of God, it is important to settle a few points first about the nature of recognizing truth. We can come to the knowledge of truth in at least a few different ways. We can find out truth through:

1. the *rational mind* (through logic, reason, and thinking);
2. our *empirical senses* (through physical senses of hearing, sight, taste, touch, and smell); and
3. our *subjective experiences* (through memory, experience, and emotion).

These three faculties could be considered *knowledge sensors*. As far as I can tell, it is through each sensor individually or in cooperation that truth could ever be recognized and the world properly understood.

You might think, out of the three sensors listed, that it would be the empirical senses that would be the most important way to know truth. After all, it is commonly believed that if someone can't see or physically experience something, then how can they know it exists? However, out of these three sensors, it is probably the rational mind that is our most basic tool in the pursuit of any claim to truth. It is through your rational mind that all other sensors are interpreted to be meaningful.

For example, when you see a table in front of you and place your hands upon it, the mind registers what the eyes are seeing and the hands are feeling. The experience of that object is being passed on to the brain, notifying you about the shape and hardness of the table. In such a case, sight and touch serve as instruments in enabling a reasoned understanding of the true nature of the table and your relationship toward it. Thus, it is by reason and logic that you develop a true understanding of what is experienced all around you.

Many philosophers believe that, because our reason and senses can at times be unreliable, we therefore cannot trust them in providing for us any certainty of truth. To some degree, they do have a point. It is true that senses can give us impressions that don't really exist. Think of the mirage in the desert. To our visual perception (empirical senses) there appears to be a body of water in the distance; yet, upon closer investigation, the "water" ends up being just the heat waves rising from the sand—our sight seemed to has deceived us.

Likewise, the unreliability of our ability to reason can be easily demonstrated—just think of the last time you made a poor choice under intense stress. Poor choices are often made in times when we experience high external and emotional pressures. This pressure clouds our clarity of mind and limits our ability to think, clearly rendering our reason less effective. So it is without doubt a true statement that, in some ways, even our mind can deceive us.

So what are we to do? Are we to give up and admit that nothing can be ultimately known? Absolutely not! If reason and the senses cannot be reliable at all, then we could never trust any scientific facts since scientific facts are ultimately dependant upon a scientist's reason and senses in the first place! Despite the times when occasional self-deceptions do occur (like objects seeming to bend in the water), most times we are only momentarily deceived. Instead of discarding all senses and reason as untrustworthy, we can still trust them, providing that we are keenly aware of the potential illusions that could exist and learn from them. In using our sensors, we can discern what is true, and therefore they are generally reliable with an extremely high degree of accuracy.

In other words, we can learn from our past experiences and avoid being tricked in the future. After a deceptive experience with a mirage, one now has the knowledge to avoid that deception in the future. Likewise, after making bad choices in the heat of the moment, experience and reason teach us that we must wait until anger subsides before making important choices. In this way, we can avoid being tricked in the same way again and grow in experiential wisdom.

The "I Don't Believe What I Can't See" Fallacy

An influential group of scientists, teachers, and philosophers tend to promote the widespread idea that unless our senses of touch, sight, hearing, taste, and smell are able to experience something, it doesn't exist—this is called empiricism.

At its very infancy, this worldview fails in two important ways. First, any statement that says something to the effect of "unless I can use my senses to perceive it, I don't believe it to be true" itself could never be physically verified. They are making knowledge claims about only knowing truth by the senses in a statement that is created through their reason with concepts that exist beyond their senses! This statement is a truth statement that could never be "seen" or "touched," and so according its own criteria, it fails and is self-defeating.

The second reason why it fails is because it begins with the false assumption that anything that exists must be sensed; and since our soul or God is beyond the senses, we must then conclude that He could never be known to exist. However, as we have seen, empirical sense alone is not our foundational sense for perceiving reality—this foundation belongs to the rational mind. Suffice it to say, at this point in time, the "I don't believe what I can't see" idea is fallacious—a fallacy in which all truth is being placed neatly into a physically manageable box, where anything outside of it is assumed to be impossible to know.

As valuable as empirical science is, we must be aware that the scientific method is limited in its ability to recognize every truth. *In the areas of truth where touch and sight are ineffective, we have no choice but to rely upon the rational mind, which carries the unique ability of being independent of the other senses in discerning truth.* Using the rational mind is the main sensor that will be used to recognize the existence of God.

Discovering Truth Beyond Science

As I have hinted, certain things are well beyond the scope of any scientific method to prove—some of those things are automatically believed and yet are still completely rational. I'm willing to bet that you believe that other people possess minds similar to yours—the fact that you are reading my thoughts prove this assumption. In this way, you naturally assume that other minds similar to your own have their own distinct consciousnesses and sets of ideas. By assuming this belief, you are actually behaving in a perfectly reasonable and rational way. It's a form of basic common sense.

But let's think about this belief for a minute—is there any way to prove *scientifically* that other minds truly do exist? After all, isn't it possible that, right now, you are actually an avatar living in a matrix-type holographic world where loved ones are mere characters that you digitally interact with? It could be that you have been heavily drugged and your life is just a product of a comatose hallucination. Or perhaps we are all just characters in a dream you are having while you lie unconscious in a hospital somewhere due to an unfortunate accident. Aren't these scenarios possible?

My point is that there is no scientific way to show you that other people are not just illusions inside your head. It is a natural instinct of pure rational faith to assume that other minds are in existence all around you, so much so that you live with this assumption in place without a second thought. It is a justified belief and doesn't need any explanation or deeper thought. The "other minds dilemma" is an example of you making a reasonable faith-based assumption without any scientific evidence to back it up. To believe in other minds is a statement of faith—but a rational one at that.

Another obvious certainty that we hold to by faith is the assumption that the world existed before we were born. The day that you came to first understand something about this world is the day that you also subconsciously acknowledged that the world had already been in existence long before your birth. This is a perfectly rational belief—another rational statement of faith.

But the problem arises again: how do you know this to be true? Where are the scientific facts? After all, you could not experience the world empirically before you were born to verify that it didn't just pop into existence at the same time you did. For all you know, there may have been nothing at all until you arrived; and then all things were brought about at the same time! You can't even prove that the world didn't pop into existence in the last 15 minutes either, because it is possible that memories could have been suddenly programmed along with the illusion of age and erosion assigned to the world. All previous documents and photos of the past could have been forged, all for the purpose of deceiving you—a Truman Show-type experience.

Yet even without any sort of verifiable proof, it can still be assumed, by a reasonable faith, that the world existed long before you came into being. Anything contrary seems to be a violation of our common sense—an unnecessary philosophical distraction.

This type of reasonable faith can be applied to numerous immaterial categories of truth outside the verification of science. Truths such as love, the past, historical events, mathematics, logic, inspiration, good and evil, God, consciousness, the soul, and artistic vision are such examples. For the greater part of our lives, we live as faith-based creatures resting comfortably in many basic unempirical foundations.

If we cannot prove something with empirical science, does this make our belief irrational? On the contrary—it does not. Science isn't sufficient to explain the fullness of what we experience in reality. Our senses naturally presuppose many things without the need for proof or justification. We must understand that science in and of itself is simply an aid to understanding some truths, but not all truth. For many immaterial aspects of our lives, science is in fact useless—in these places, we are creatures of instinctual faith.

Belief in God is a Basic Belief

As we have seen, mankind effortlessly trusts in many things that are void of any evidence because we are wired to take certain obvious truths for granted. Now, the question we should ask is: "Is God a basic belief in a similar way that other minds might be?" Since basic beliefs are, by nature, self-evident and justified, since they best represent reality, then I believe that God not only fits into this category but is the most reasonable explanation for why we are programmed in this way in the first place.

All people, to some degree, are very much aware of the purposeful designs that make up the very substance of our natural world. Ecosystems carry the necessary life that allows for it to work—without the creature-to-creature, and creature-to-plant relationships, serious damage would occur to the system as a whole.

Thus, symbiotic relationships within the animal kingdom maintain the survival of numerous species. The clownfish and sea anemone relationship is a popular example of this type of symbiotic relationship. A clownfish will live in the tentacles of the sea anemone all its life and, because the anemone's tentacles sting other fish that get too close to it, the clownfish becomes protected from its fishy predators. On the other hand, a butterfly fish will attempt to eat the sea anemone's tentacles and kill it, but because the clownfish will attack and defend the anemone from these predators, the anemone is safe. Both animals inevitably benefit from their mutual relationship.

Now, in taking this example into account (and numerous other examples could be used), I would argue that God is a basic belief in the minds of mankind, as they hypothesize why purpose is found everywhere in the natural world. This supernatural agent is assumed to have been responsible for wondrously complex design—that Being is that which cultures would generically call God.

Even in a culture influenced by atheistic thought, the "appearance" of design in the natural world is widely acknowledged to be true. On top of this, many atheist science professors will inconsistently speak and teach as though there are divine intentions imprinted within the natural world by using language that only fits within the framework of theism (belief in God). Textbooks and day-to-day conversations will often state the "purpose" and "reason" of biological functions or laws of nature, even though the atheistic universe is completely void of both.

So it is here, even in the worldview of atheism, that we can still see an all-too-human faith that sees a purpose and intent behind the natural world. If that purpose were to be acknowledged and traced back, it would logically lead even the most hardened yet honest atheist to admit that a Being must exist in order to provide purpose in the first place. In this way, just as basic beliefs are necessary frameworks for all understanding, the concept of a personal Creator can be easily added to the list of foundational beliefs.

An Instinct for Eternity: Ethical Principles

Another point that gives support to God being a basic rational belief is our eternal-mindedness. We live in constant tension between *living in the finite* and *living for the infinite*. Often, we find ourselves fighting morally uphill battles pondering whether to obey our inner "principles." By pondering these inner moral principles, we naturally direct ourselves to the unseen guidelines of a higher reality.

Unfortunately, the choice is often made to ignore morals, because maintaining them can become costly. For example, imagine you unjustly received a $200 speeding ticket from a police officer. Knowing that you are innocent, you are inclined to fight this ticket. However, once you calculated the cost of the legal struggle which would ensue (taking time off work, the travel expenses to get to court, the lawyer fees, etc.), you determine payment of the ticket is cheaper and easier than paying the several hundred dollars it would cost for the legal battle.

But even when this happens to others, there is a lingering sense that something moral is at stake. Instead of making the payment, you then decide to fight this wrongful offense, accepting the personal loss as a worthy sacrifice for defending the higher moral principle. In this way, you fought the injustice for, "the principle of the thing."

Throughout life, many situations such as these arise where attempts for personal vindication, honor, dignity, and justice manifests. In these cases, it ought to be obvious that *we are fighting for an otherworldly ideal with an eternal focus*—a focus that is perfectly consistent in a worldview where God and His objective ethical standard exists.

An Instinct for Eternity: Pleasure

The tension between the *temporal* and the *eternal* is why many people may also choose to live in the pursuit of *pleasure*. We desire ultimate personal satisfaction. Obsessive addictions to porn, drugs (illegal and prescription), alcohol, social media, fighting, gambling, sex, honor, fame, music, performance, acceptance, video games, novels, self-inflicted pain, movies, and the power of the occult become temporary fixes and cheap replacements for true, long-lasting personal satisfaction and happiness.

We long for more than this world can offer us. The physical world cannot satisfy us, and so is it reasonable to conclude that we are lacking something else—something that exists beyond the physical—something that we are missing that can satisfy our inner longings. If we were to receive all the fame, fortune, money, and sex we could handle, it would never be enough. Once we get bored with that, it would be quickly replaced with some other temporary pleasure. This problem indicates that people are inwardly searching for the joyful satisfaction that they were designed for that will completely fill the void or emptiness—not temporarily, but permanently.

Again, this is all perfectly consistent in a world where we have been created for something eternal—some source of divine need that exists beyond sense perception.

The Pitfalls of Naturalism

In a godless universe, meaning or purpose at best become self-invented illusions used to make life more bearable in a depressingly purposeless world. The more reasonable explanation for why we are aware of our own purpose and meaning in life is that it is actually not illusory at all, but rather an intentional part of our subconscious makeup given to us by Something.

Meaning and purpose exist as driving forces for all of life. Every action that you do and choice that you make is already assumed to be meaningful and purposeful to you, otherwise you wouldn't do it. If we are to be consistent, the natural driving force of purposefulness makes the most sense only if we accept that a personal God exists who creates with purpose and meaning in mind.

The fact that God created us for a purpose is implied in understanding that we are objects of His creation. Nothing gets created without a reason or purpose behind it. If we took away the natural assumption that people have of purposefulness and meaningfulness, and replaced these thoughts with naturalistic purposelessness and futility in our educational centers, what would we culturally expect to happen in a few generations? Is it reasonable to expect greater manifestations of confusion, selfishness, and anger as people inwardly attempt to deal with the implications of having no ultimate purpose in the universe? Is it likely that we would anticipate a whole spectrum of unfortunate generational effects ranging from depression, to anxiety, to suicide, to various forms of bitter violence, bullying, and pointless school shootings? Absolutely! In a God-less (and thus purposeless) society, we should not be surprised when horrific lawless events increase, as people attempt to live out life as they choose to see fit. If nothing really matters at the end of the day anyway—if there are no real eternal consequences for my actions except for the impending nothingness that comes with death—then the violent "survival of the fittest" mentality consistently fits the worldview.

This is where naturalism lacks a rational foundation. We naturally understand that anything with purposeful function must have been crafted by an intelligent source with purposeful intent in mind. Everything that we have in our physical body has a purpose, so why wouldn't we expect to have been also purposefully designed in whole?

It is here that the rationality of a natural belief in God over atheism is revealed, in that we naturally recognize that life produces life, intelligence produces intelligence, and personality produces personality; scientifically speaking, we have never seen anything contrary to these patterns before. We have never seen non-life create living things nor impersonal things create anything intelligent or personal. In light of this reasoning, the most basic conclusion mankind has traditionally come to about the purposeful world is that a living, intelligent, and personal Being must have been responsible.

Atheism is revealed in this way to be a groundless leap of faith into a world of imaginative speculation. Atheism must inevitably come to rely upon unobservable and irrational doctrines such as: randomness creating order, non-living matter producing life, non-intelligence producing intelligence, and that purposeless forces and matter somehow gave way to personal consciousness, and so on. In this fundamental way, atheism is not at all scientific, since it gives answers that don't match the observational and scientifically testable groundwork for what we see in the world today.

Could Chance Do It?

The atheistic explanation of how a universe with "apparent" design came about is through random natural mechanisms according to "chance." Atheism posits that when left to chance, and given enough time, anything can happen, including the appearance of complex designs in nature such as an animal's cell. This, unfortunately, is a misunderstanding of what chance actually is.

Chance is really just a word used to describe mathematical probabilities—what are the odds are of a coin being tossed a certain number of times and falling on heads versus tails, for example. *Chance has no mechanical power or ability to create anything at all*, and adding time to the mix doesn't help very much either.

Time is just the duration in which something *could* be done in. Using the term time and chance as explanations for design, for example the first life on Earth, actually provides no clear explanation at all; *what is required for life is not chance or time but the necessary conditions.* I'll give an atheist all the time and chance they want, but if those conditions for life are not there, then their worldview comes to a dead end, and fast.

For instance, let's say a galaxy-sized tornado has existed for 900 billion years with an unlimited number of prepped and ready car particles flying through it non-stop—all the elements needed to assemble a single type of car. Imagine that the elements of steel, glass, rubber, oil, gasoline, glass, cable, etc. are all gently colliding together with each other in this massive, moving tornado. Even with this material, time, and random movements, this tornado would never be able to:

1. Assemble the *appropriate shapes and sizes* needed for the requirements of the car.
2. Assemble any of *the complex parts necessary* for any *purposeful function* such as alternators, pistons, fuses, tires, and electrical panels.
3. Arrange and *attach car parts in an orderly fashion* to create a fully functional and operational car.

It is absurd to assume that something purposeful will come about by random chance, or even favorable conditions, without some sort of intelligent mind behind it. The mathematical probability of such a claim would be too absurd to *rationally* believe.

Randomness never produces complex order; there is no system of laws in the universe that we know of where this is even possible—creations such as cars can only be made by the hand of an intelligent agent aided by the right tools under the right conditions. How much more would that be true for the ultra complexity of living creatures, ecosystems, or human beings with a thinking consciousness and intelligence? Isn't it therefore extremely reasonable that for most of history, when gazing upon a purposeful world, the vast majority of mankind came to the sensible conclusion that previous intelligence accounts for all the purposeful things that we witness?

With all that has been considered, the question that really ought to be asked is whether the burden of proof rests upon those who believe in God (the theists), or those who deny this naturally basic and rational belief (the atheists)? I think it's the atheists that have some explaining to do.

What Do Christians Have to Prove?

Some tend to think that, since followers of Christ are making the claim for God, the burden of proof must fall upon their shoulders. Some state that "the absence of evidence is the evidence of absence," but as we have clearly seen (in the "other minds dilemma"), the absence of evidence is not necessarily the evidence of absence. There are many things that cannot be scientifically verified but are nevertheless true.

First, we must ask the question as to whether the scientific method is qualified enough to provide proof for the existence of anything that lacks physical properties, such as God. Is it rational to think that we can observe immaterial things such as love, consciousness, the laws of logic, or God under a microscope? Or how about charting their pH levels on a graph? The answer is an obvious no. It is irrational to assume that God can be scientifically tested or proven when He is a disembodied mind outside the physical world. God, by definition, is "*supernatural*" (beyond nature); therefore, God cannot be subjected to physical testing. For a person to ask a Christian to provide scientific evidence for God is to ask a fallacious question, making a category mistake.

Looking within the universe for proof of God is like staring intently into a painting in the hopes of discovering the artist who painted it in the painting itself. The artist, of course, cannot be found in the painting, because the painting is a creation that already implies the painter was present at some point—even if you never saw them.

The art enables a person to make a few factual assumptions about an artist. For instance, when observing an art piece, a person can reasonably assume that the artist possesses a level of creativity, that there is an understanding of beauty and orderliness in design. It is assumed also that the artist must possess some sort of technical ability, along with helpful tools that assist in getting his imaginative thoughts onto the canvas effectively. Similarly, within our own created universe, we are able to have our own drawn-out assumptions about the Creator. (We will explore this in more detail in chapters 2 and 3).

Our proof for God is not in physical science but an investigation into forensic science, mathematical probability, and the historical sciences, which are different types of science altogether. We are looking back at the prospect of various creatures in their orderly design and, by using our reason, connect the dots, as a detective would follow the clues to build a concrete case at a crime scene.

This can be done with very little effort on the theist's behalf. If I were to glance outside my window and notice that the fallen leaves under my tree form the words "I love you" on the lawn, I wouldn't need to conduct a scientific investigation and spend my time theorizing as to how this came to be through natural processes. Instead, I can rationally assume that an intelligent source (the most likely culprit would be my wife) had placed them there with the purpose of communicating a message of affection to me. Reasonable, isn't it? Likewise, we can look and see that a combination of the design, purpose, and information that is laid out all around us points to the conclusion that our world originated from someone extremely intelligent.

The Atheist's Burden

It seems to me, therefore, that it is the atheist and not the theist who bears the burden of proof for the extraordinary claim that a non-intelligent matter-based origin of the universe gave way to intelligence and immaterial truths. It is up to the atheist to come up with a rational alternative for the widespread common-sense belief of an intelligent influence behind the finely tuned complexities of our planet. They must attempt to remove or explain away the basic faith-based belief that has been inherent within mankind since the beginning of culture.

We know scientifically that only life produces other life—this is observed and documented; therefore it can be considered to be a scientific fact. But if one chooses to theorize that life arose from non-living chemicals alongside cosmic displays of energy, as the naturalist would assume, then that view first requires evidence of some kind in order for it to be rationally held.

The Christian Advantage

It is interesting to note that the believer in God (the theist) has the scientific and philosophical upper hand in considering explanations for truth. Unlike the naturalist, the theistic worldview is able to take us beyond the natural world for answers.

In naturalism, there is only one source for truth—the physical. In Christianity, however, we can look at two possible sources for truth—the first being physical causes; the second being supernatural causes.

Science—like a compass—must have the ability to freely point in the right direction unhindered so that we can explore every possible avenue for answers. We must go where the evidence leads us, and if that is to the supernatural world and the written revelation of God, then so be it.

It is also interesting to note that almost every major department of science—chemistry, oceanography, biology, genetics, and quantum theory—was either founded or pioneered in a major way by Christians or other theists. Even the founder of the modern scientific method, Francis Bacon (1561-1626), was a devoted Anglican Christian, who wrote in *Essays, Civil and Moral* that, "a little philosophy inclineth man's mind to atheism, but in depth philosophy bringeth men's minds about to religion." Christians are not against science or natural explanations in any way, but people committed to the possibility of two avenues of explanation and one goal—to see how God created this world.

We are indebted to numerous theists who have made paradigm shifts in their particular fields. Sir Isaac Newton, Johannes Kepler, Rene Descartes, Robert Boyle, and Albert Einstein are a few of the major players in many scientific advancements and much of the background stimulation for their scientific curiosities and contributions to the current state of scientific affairs was directed by an inner desire to know how God designed His world. Historically, they are not alone, since God has been a major motivational factor responsible for lifting science off the ground and providing the necessary foundations for scientists today to work from.

Into the Revelation of God

Even though I am convinced that the common knowledge of God is ingrained into our nature and does not need proof in order to be considered justified as a rational belief, I have still chosen to take the liberty of making a rational case for the Triune God of the Christian faith.

In discovering how the Christian faith is rational, you can trace the logic through a few basic steps. Step 1 guides us with a foundational question: *In examining nature and mankind, is the evidence for God a reasonable one?* What can be known about Him in the natural world without the Bible? If it is reasonable that God is evident through the testimony of the natural world, then Step 2 continues into another question: *Since God does exist, is it reasonable to conclude that He has revealed Himself to mankind? If so, how could we know it to be true?* Since God then exists, which of the religions (if any) is the right one, and how could we know for sure God has written anything for us? What characteristics or credentials should that revelation possess? Once these questions have been answered then the final step is Step 3, which deals with the question: *Since God has spoken to us, is it reasonable to ignore what He had to say to us?* What does He expect of us? What does He want us to know? How does He want us to then live?

All of these steps should be presupposed in the three conditions for the best worldview that we earlier spoke about: it must be reasonably sound, consistent in basic life's experience, and practical and livable. Reasonable. Consistent. Practical.

These questions may seem mysterious to you at this point, so allow me to lead you in seeking out the answers. Let us first begin in the realm of natural theology.

2
Observational Demonstrations
OF GOD'S GLORY

But I may say that the impossibility of conceiving that this grand and wondrous universe, with our conscious selves, arose through chance, seems to me the chief argument for the existence of God.

CHARLES DARWIN, IN A LETTER TO D.H. DOEDES, APRIL 2, 1873

And he made from one man every nation of mankind to live on all the face of the earth, having determined allotted periods and the boundaries of their dwelling place, that they should seek God, and perhaps feel their way toward him and find him. Yet he is actually not far from each one of us.

ACTS 17:26-27

The Cosmological Witness

As we have alluded to previously, God's existence screams through the fabric of purpose-filled design, and our universe is ripe with this observation. The first of these testimonies we are going to examine is in the phenomena of motions and causes.

Everything that makes up the physical universe—gases, liquids, energy, light, planets, life, and stars—can be defined as contingent things. A contingent thing is anything that has depended or is currently depending upon outside causes for its own existence. In other words, a contingent thing is something finite that has had a beginning and is subject to the scientific laws of cause and effect.

Let's take a single seed as an example. A seed exists due to the previous cause that came before it—the parent plant that produced the seed. The parent plant produced the seed, thus it is the cause for the seed's existence. And the parent plant itself came from a plant before it, and so on. The trail of causes will continue on backward in time until you get to that original first cause. Just as seeds and plants are contingent, so are all the physical things in the universe dependent upon their own previous causes.

Consider now an energy-based example: a person might ask, "What is the cause of the heat on Earth?" We could answer that the solar flares from the sun coming through space causes the heat on Earth.

Another question could then be asked: "What caused those solar flares from the sun?" We could answer that the solar flares are due to the explosions on the sun's surface.

An additional question would result: "What is the cause for the explosions on the sun?" The answer would be that the explosions on the sun's surface are caused when the sun's gases are ignited.

The next question would be: "How did this ignition from the gases happen?"

Over and over, we could look deeper into the past of every contingent thing and find more causes and answers to our "why" questions. We could keep probing deeper into the depths of the past to uncover more explanations; however, this probing cannot go on forever. Even if we knew all the causes, we would eventually need to arrive at the very beginning of all causes and effects—the very first Cause of all contingent things.

What was this very first cause that sparked all other contingent things to come into existence? Reason follows that, since everything in the universe is contingent, something must exist that is non-contingent and ontologically necessary for everything physical. Something beyond the physical needed to always exist in order to create the physical. This is the conclusion we must ultimately come to when considering the causal effects of contingent things in the universe—a timeless Uncaused Causer of all things exists.

Proof for the Beginning: Expanding Stars

The physical universe also bears evidence of a beginning. One piece of scientific data that supports the beginning of the universe is a breakthrough observation that has been made with the Hubble telescope. It has been revealed that millions of stars and galaxies in the universe are moving outwards, expanding deeper into the empty space beyond. This implies that, in the past, the stars were much closer together, expanding from an unknown point of origin.

Though scientifically problematic in many areas, a common theory suggested by many astronomers is that, in the past, there was a cosmic "Big Bang," where all that currently exists was suddenly brought into being from some point of explosive singularity in the past. According to this theory, after the big bang was ignited, all the chaotic collisions of atoms brought about the order that we see today over billions of years.

I don't disagree that the stars are expanding; but I hold to the book of Genesis' account for the origin of all temporal things, because the Bible is reliable and inspired (something that we will cover later on). In the scripture, the beginning of the universe was documented to have been brought into existence through divine origin in a miraculous, well-ordered, and matured creation. Where the Bible differs fundamentally from the Big Bang theory is that the Big Bang theory assumes order came about by a microscopically-explosive, chaotic point of origin. In the historical scripture, God reveals that He created all things in six days, orchestrated by God's supernatural hand a relatively short time ago. It takes far less faith for me to believe in the Bible's observationally consistent account of an orderly world than our latest popular theory.

Yet, even in the Big Bang model, an initial immaterial cause would still be necessary in order to initiate, from nothing, the explosion required to make up the universe and the conscious beings like us that live in it. In speaking of this idea, the famous scientist Stephen Hawking even maintained that "it would be very difficult to explain why the universe should have begun in just this way, except as the act of a God who intended to create beings like us."[1]

Proof for the Beginning: The Second Law

A second scientific proof that the universe is not eternal but had a beginning is found in the Second Law of Thermodynamics, which states that in a closed system (such as the universe) all usable energy is decreasing—not being destroyed, but winding down, turning from order toward chaos and disorder.

Our sun and stars are decreasing in both light and energy, which can be observed by the fading of color and brightness of stars over time. Many dying, exploding stars called super-novas have been documented, showing us that their life in the cosmos is running out. Interestingly enough, no stars have ever been observed to form in the universe—star formation is highly theorized, but not verified, which itself testifies to this second law.

Cosmic evolution attempts to teach us that all things are moving from disorder into recognizable patterns and order arranged into stable bodies, but the evidence seems to be pointing in the opposite direction. The once-ordered cosmos is *tending toward* disorder and chaos, chemicals are becoming unstable and corroding, metals rusts away by erosion, mate-rials wear out, bodies weaken over time—all things act as though, at some point in time, they were structured or "wound up" with the appropriate amount of sustainable energy needed. Now, all we see is the universal sign of all things inevitably run-ning their course toward disorder.

Three Possible Conclusions for the Universe's Origin

There are only three possible explanations for the origin of the orderly physical universe. First, that the universe was *self-caused;* second, that the universe was *caused by nothing* at all; or third, that the universe was *caused by someone* with an initiative beyond the universe itself.

The first possibility of the universe being self-caused is obviously impossible since nothing can ever be self-caused. For something to be self-caused, it would need to exist already—prior to its own existence—in order to cause itself. This is impossible, because in order for me to create myself, I would need to exist earlier than my own existence in order to do it! This is logically absurd and obviously unworkable.

Secondly, to believe that nothing caused our universe is equally impossible. After all, "nothing" is by definition just that—nothing—not a thing at all. Where nothing is, there can be no matter, no energy—just a void, dark, empty space of nothingness. Nothing is the opposite of existence; for one to exist, the other cannot at the same time in the same way. If there was ever nothing, then it is impossible that something could result from it, because there is no force to create anything. If there were ever a time when nothing existed then there would continue to be nothing still, for nothingness has no potential to create anything.

Someone Beyond the Physical Universe

The last explanation remains the most logical and valid possibility—that the universe must be caused by a previous intelligence and power. The other views are simply not possible.

One might object at this point and ask why it must be that the first cause needs to be a person? Doesn't there require only something as the first cause to create the universe and not necessarily a personal someone like God? The problem with an impersonal thing being responsible for our universe is that the impersonal things we see today (objects, energies, powers, forces, and so forth) don't have any creative ability to bring about many of the designed complexities that we see today. The nature of something that is purposeful and complex puts strict guidelines upon what exactly has the potential to create it. Mysteries such as molecular life, biology, and personal consciousness are far too advanced for random accidents to achieve even if guided by a host of numerous eternal forces—intelligence is a foundational requirement for complex, intricate creations.

Another reason as to why the original Cause must be personal is that, for our universe to come into existence, the originator of it would need to establish the first act in the first creative moment. This can be accomplished only through a personal God exercising His *free will* in order to take the first decisive step in creating something.

Even the natural laws themselves require an explanation since the laws are mathematically precise and—as far as we know—unchanging. What set them up this way? What keeps them continuously stable? What set them up to be the rules that all other physical things must be governed by, if not by a personal and calculating God capable of arranging stability in the physical world? For the laws of nature to exist, something must also continue to impose the regularity of these laws upon our active universe—something that is keeping them regular in their continuous action, strength, and circuits. Physicist Richard Morris said that the strength of each of nature's forces "...must have just the right strength if there is to be any possibility of life. For example, if electrical forces were much stronger than they are, then no element heavier than hydrogen could form... but electrical repulsion cannot be too weak. If it were, protons could combine too easily, and the sun (assuming that it had somehow managed to exist up to now) would explode like a thermo-nuclear bomb."[2] The physical constants are therefore effectually "finely tuned," which is best explained by the genius of a Supreme Mind.

What Then Created God?

If God created everything, and everything needs a cause, then wouldn't it follow that God would also need a cause? So what caused God?

This is a common question from both Christians and non-Christians, and it is indeed a fair one. However, this problem's answer has to do with a misunderstanding of the nature of God. The question itself is erroneous since the question assumes a *changing* God—a god that is subjected to the causal laws of the physical universe.

God—as defined by the follower of Christ—is an eternal Being, unchanging in essence and character, with an immaterial Spirit. God is not subject to same physical or natural laws that He uses for the functioning of His own universe! It is only *contingent* things that require an outside cause because they are subject to the law of causality in the material world. God is not in that category of contingency or subject to any causes but His own pleasure.

God carries a *necessary* existence that lives beyond the parameters of contingencies such as time, space, and matter. There would have to be a God who exists outside of time and is eternal in order to form the things that are finite. Therefore, the Creator is not only necessary for all existence, but He is *eternally self-existent in and of Himself*, truly enjoying an undisturbed freedom from anything. In short, nothing caused God to exist, because He is beyond causal reach. He couldn't have had a cause for His existence because He is the one who created the laws of cause and effect in the first place!

God Best Explains the Origin of the Universe

Contrary to the old mythical fables, God is no bearded old man in the clouds—this would be idolatry. God is an eternally self-existent, all-powerful intelligence with unlimited capabilities in creative potential and wonder. God exists far beyond our world and exists in a superior state (transcendence), living above and beyond this material plane. He is a Being, the Source for all other sources, the Uncaused Cause, the Necessary One, and the Everlasting Creator. This is the Lord Almighty.

The alternative view that all things happened by random chance is simply the "god of the gaps" for naturalistic explanations. This theory explains little scientifically and is in conflict with the observable scientific evidences that we have just looked at. For the rational person seeking to know why there is something rather than nothing at all, God is his best explanation.

The *Teleological* Witness

Regardless of the worldview that a person possesses, the appearance of design and purposefulness in the world is an undisputable fact. In the secular scientific communities, this allusion to the design-like qualities of nature is called "The Anthropic Principle." Earth in particular beautifully displays a most vivid network of very complex and fine-tuned factors, all of which are set up perfectly to make it possible for life to exist and survive. This testimony to the design of the natural world is what I mean when I refer to the *teleological* witness.

Scientifically speaking, we know that life hangs delicately in the balance by numerous variables and environmental factors, all of which we call *constants*. Variables such as the precise force of Earth's gravity, electromagnetism, the mass density in the universe, the expansion rate of the universe, our solar system's position in the galaxy, and Earth's perfect air mixture are some of these important considerations that enable us to be aware that we are indeed a "Goldilocks" planet. Earth is perfectly set to life's necessary *pre-conditions*.

If something were to change these conditions (some even in the slightest degree), life would not be able to exist on Earth at all. This is the very reason why humans are currently seeking other planets to inhabit, because we believe that due to the continuous changes in our planet's characteristics and declining natural resources, that Earth will one day lack those necessary pre-conditions for life. With these meticulously-tuned factors, one could rationally suspect that Earth has been set up as a sort of "natural preserve" governed by God, who uses natural law for the express purpose of creating a normative living habitation for animals and humans.

To own a Venus flytrap, a host of pre-conditions must first be met to promote the plant's health and well-being. You need the right temperature, amount of light, watering method, bugs to feed it, etc. If you fail in any one of these areas, it cannot survive. Its fragile little life hangs delicately in the balance of its surroundings—surroundings that must be perfectly staged. So it is with *all* life on Earth. Robert Jastrow, the head of NASA's Goddard Institute for Space Studies, referred to the evidence of intelligent design in the universe as "the most powerful evidence for the existence of God ever to come out of science."[3] In a forensic sense, these interconnected natural constants carry a weighty argument for a divine gardener in our midst.

The Miracle of "Simple" Life

The natural constants are only part of the bigger picture. They are so tuned that probability makes it impossible to suggest that these factors could have arisen from naturalistic, unguided processes. Furthermore, could life ever have truly arrived without the aid of intelligent intervention? Naturalists seem to think so. However, that idea is being challenged by thousands of scientists. It has been shown by biochemist Michael Behe that the complexity of even the most basic of molecular machines, such as the bacterial flagellum, are advanced, *irreducibly complex* biological machines.

Some eukaryotic cells in your body have what is called a filament—a tail-like ligament that is used to propel itself around its environment (like the tail on a sperm cell or a tadpole). It can be observed under the microscope, at the base where the filament meets the cell wall, that both gears and rotary-motor mechanisms are clearly visible! Mechanical devices inside a living thing! This creature is wonderfully crafted with mechanical components—this creature is a biological machine!

If you take away one gear or compromise the filament's rotary system, then the bacterial flagellum could not propel itself for survival. What car could complete its purpose if the starter, battery, or alternator were removed? It would not function properly at all.

Your body likewise is a well-crafted biological machine with custom-made designer parts that work similarly to how any other machine would. At this very moment, the cells within our body exist as miniature biological units (like the bacterial flagellum), each equipped with an organic-based assembly line for making thousands of necessary proteins for your survival. If you were to walk into a car factory today, you would see an assembly line with numerous machines, each creating and assembling parts for the purpose of creating a whole vehicle. The cells in your body do the same thing, only with proteins! You literally have little factories within you created for the purpose of prolonging life and producing what your body needs to stay alive.

The worst thing to happen to naturalism has been the invention of the microscope, whereby we can now see that blood is not just a simple blob of tissue as was once thought. Instead, blood contains a literal world of biologically-complex machinery that defies scientific naturalism and shakes the theory to its very core. How could natural, unguided processes account for the complexity of your cells? Cells are so complex that even the atheistic microbiologist Michael Denton admits, "The complexity of the simplest known type of cell is so great that it is impossible to accept that such an object could have been thrown together suddenly by some kind of freakish, vastly improbable event. Such an occurrence would be indistinguishable from a miracle."[4] This naturalist's statement is one of scientific common sense.

Could Living Cells Evolve?

When I speak of evolution, I am speaking not of *microevolution*, which covers gradual changes within a given animal family, such as the cat or dog family. This type of evolution is observational and testable, which is the hallmark of true science and cannot be rationally denied. Instead, when I speak of evolution,

I am speaking about the widespread belief of macroevolution and its claim that life gradually changes over millions of years from simpler animals into more complex ones.

Many suppose this to be the case, yet there seems to be a problem with this theory even on the smallest level. During the time scale that evolution requires, the cell wouldn't realistically have been able to live long enough between any major evolutionary development that is essential for survival. This is one of main problems that evolution must answer.

One example is the cell's reproductive ability. In order for the first living cell to survive it must be immediately equipped with the ability to quickly replicate and divide itself. It would need the necessary functioning parts that would enable this process to take place at the very outset of its life, which would—according to evolution theory—have taken too long to develop. During this waiting period, the cell would have long since died out before it was able to form the ability to replicate, thus ending its survival and existence almost immediately. Assuming evolution was possible, without this ability to immediately divide, evolution is a pointless and fruitless process. This is just one of the countless issues of cellular necessities that evolutionists must come to terms with—natural processes cannot create the type of complexity needed at the very beginning of the cellular lifespan.

Just as with the bacterial flagellum, the cell needs a set of basic pieces to have been assembled together at its very beginning in order for the cell to function properly. It had to have been built all at once by a Grand Designer, since evolving piece by piece through a blind process would have led to its destruction from the cell's very conception.

Additionally, all the parts of the cell do their different tasks efficiently in orchestrated unison to the aid of the healthy cell and the benefit of the whole animal. The living cell is undoubtedly a concentrated miracle of the micro-world.

Humans, on a much larger scale, have a seemingly endless array of numerous mechanical body parts such as springs (the organ of Corti), heart valves (mitral, tricuspid, aortic, pulmonary), lubricators (tear glands, saliva, mucus, sexual fluids), and filters (liver, kidneys, nose hair)—all of which testify to the glory of the intricate design of a God with immeasurable amounts of knowledge.

Consider just the human hand alone, with all of its perfections and abilities for our advantage. Leonardo da Vinci dissected bodies in a cathedral while working on human anatomy, and he skillfully illustrated in great detail the inner workings of the hand. For him, the hand was seen to be the most versatile instrument on Earth, and we use it almost thoughtlessly every day!

What about the human eye? This is an organ that could never function unless fully developed at once. The eye is designed with 130 million light-sensitive rods and cones, which generate photochemical reactions that convert light into electrical impulses. They are equipped with an automatically-adjusting camera lens, complete with automatic aiming, focus, aperture control, cleaning (tears), and maintenance while the eyelids are closed when sleeping. Does it make more rational sense that these irreducibly-complex instruments came about from nothing or from an intelligent God who designed them to work for our advantage?

If people have indeed evolved from a cell that lived in a chemical soup millions of years ago, then which organ evolved first? The heart, which pumps the blood and nutrients to the brain; or the brain, that informs and instructs the heart to operate? Without the heart, the brain couldn't function; yet without the brain; the heart couldn't function either—both are in a dependent relationship with each other. When one ceases to function, the other likewise has no function since one is tied to the other. They couldn't have evolved one adaptation at a time as evolution supposes, since they must be linked together for the balanced mutual support of one another. Either they appeared together at once or not at all.

Consider the necessary systems that we find in our bodies—the nervous system, digestive system, respiratory system, immune system, and reproductive system. All these unique systems function with different purposes that they have been designed with. In additional to these large systems, they are in cooperation with trillions of tiny self-directing autonomous cells, working within their own tiny cellular systems, busy balancing the chemicals of our bodies and rebuilding damaged tissue.

Even our appendix, which was once widely thought to be a vestigial organ left over from the evolutionary process, is now widely seen to possess a role in the strengthening of our immune systems.[5] Likewise, the tailbone (the coccyx) is seen in a similar way, as a leftover from evolution; but it does have a purpose in that it acts as a shock absorber when we sit down and balances out the body when we sit.[6]

In summary, we must realize that our body acts as an ecosystem of interwoven intricacies; our cells and bodily systems are like factories of biochemical machines working together simultaneously to keep us alive and functioning, and they do this without us knowing it or our approval! All these things are fully functioning in their proper place minute by minute, second by second, in wonderful harmony, fulfilling hidden beneficial purposes. How else could anyone reasonably explain this except by a Divine Engineer? I simply do not have enough faith to believe that unintelligent, blind natural occurrences are responsible for this type of complexity.

The Impotence of Naturalism

Naturalism is incapable of explaining the irreducible complexity and autonomous nature of the cells. It is equally impotent in its ability to explain how life could have arrived from non-life in the first place. *Life has only been scientifically observed to have been caused by something also in possession of the qualities of life*—a living mother gives birth to a living baby, cats breed cats, fish breed fish, dogs breed dogs, and living bacteria reproduces other living bacteria. Life creates life, period. This is observational and documentable science.

Since life has always been based out of other life forms, there is no scientific reason to expect anything to the contrary (except maybe in science fiction, I suppose). It is common to our observation; thus, this is common to rational sense. To assume that life has evolved from a few cells and added on new information over millions of years through different kinds of animals is at best imaginative—but definitely not a scientific fact. It is, at best, a wobbly scientific theory. Never has there ever been a true "missing link," nor is there a need for one, since all genetic information contained in animal life is specific and limited to each animal kind.

All living things have certain characteristics about them that are impossible for a naturalist to explain. Living bodies possess purposes in every feature—in sexual reproduction, instincts, adaptive behaviors; they even develop instinctual preparations for the future conditions of their environment.

The instinctual habit of plants and animals to plan and prepare for the future could be yet another argument that strongly supports intentional premeditative design, as opposed to randomness and natural laws. Almost every species contains at least a few instincts such as migration, hunting style, tool usage, and renovations to change their environment. Many species of bird, amphibian, and fish know instinctually after they are born where to migrate for food sources and where the mating grounds are without being previously instructed or modeled by their parents; hence, much of these behaviors are most likely instinctual (pre-programmed into their DNA "software"). No natural laws that I'm aware of can attest for this action of animals safeguarding themselves in preparation for the future without prior experiential knowledge of what they are preparing for.

Instincts, cells, organs and cravings are all non-thinking. The cell doesn't think about what it is doing. It just does its work because that's what it is designed to do—work for the organism's benefit. The intended purpose of why it does what it does lies outside of the cell itself, catalogued in the mind of God. Just as a computer game is programmed to run in a precise and productive way with their players in mind, so are animals and our bodies programmed to run in a productive, purpose-driven way. We have been "wound up" by an unseen Watchmaker, setting us up according to our biological mechanics.

What About Aliens as the Intelligent Cause for Life?

Could aliens be a possible explanation for the unique, fine-tuned features that we see in life? In recent years, a popular speculation has arisen with this view in mind called the *Panspermia Theory*. This theory states that the microorganisms of Earth may have been placed here from intelligent aliens "seeding" life at some point in the past. This theory was popularized to some degree in our contemporary time by Ridley

Scott's science fiction film *Prometheus*, where life on Earth was formed by accident via a visiting alien race.

Even though this theory is better supported than naturalistic materialism, the problem still exists that if our lives were products of alien life, the problem of causality still follows—who then designed the extraterrestrial organisms? We have the problem of causation all over again, as we found in our cosmological witness. The question would then be set back one step, but the complexity found in the extraterrestrial life would still require an explanation for itself until ultimately the Necessary Uncaused God is found. Therefore, panspermia is yet another theory that seems to be more in the arena of science fiction than based in reality; especially considering the widespread lack of scientific evidence for extraterrestrial life forms.

What Are the Odds of Life Arising by Chance?

British astrophysicist and atheist Sir Fredrick Hoyle calculated that *the probability of life arising out of organic soup by pure chance, free of any Intelligent Cause, would be one in ten to the forty thousandth power*—that is; 1 in 10 with 40,000 zeros after it! Fredrick spoke about this calculation by saying, "The likelihood of the formation of life from inanimate matter is one to a number with 40,000 naughts after it...It is big enough to bury Darwin and the whole theory of evolution. There was no primeval soup, neither on this planet nor any other, and if the beginnings of life were not random, they must therefore have been the product of purposeful intelligence." He also stated that the number 10^{40000} is "an outrageously small probability that could not be faced even if the whole universe consisted of organic soup."[7]

It is interesting to note that when dealing with any mathematical probabilities, any number that goes beyond 1 in 10 to the 50th power ($1:10^{50}$) is considered to be so far reaching that, for all practical purposes, it is impossible. In other words, the likelihood of "chance" arranging for these constants of life is not just improbable, but completely impossible hundreds of times over! Francis Crick, a promoter of the panspermia idea (that life has been seeded on Earth by extraterrestrials), has stated that "An honest man, armed with all the knowledge available to us now, could only state that, in some sense, the origin of life appears at the moment to be almost a miracle so many are the conditions which would have had to have been satisfied to get it going."[8]

The greatest mystery seems to be as to how life could have existed at all if left to randomness. In a universe where randomness is dictator, it would seem to be *far more probable that the universe should be life prohibiting*, yet it is not. Physicist P.C.W. Davies has calculated that a change in the strength of gravity or the weak force by even one part in 10^{100} would have eliminated a life-permitting universe.[9]

As scientists continue to move forward in the examination of these factors and constants, the probability of accidental design from random chance is revealing a dead hypothesis. Yet, in spite of the newest scientific discoveries about the complexity of nature of life and more additional constants, the naturalist's almighty omnipotent chance, united with randomness and time, seems to have indeed become the atheistic "god of the gaps."

In the age of the microscope, it seems rather difficult for a reasonable person to maintain the evolutionary naturalistic position. Rocket scientist (literally) Wernher von Braun said, "I find it as difficult to understand a scientist who does not acknowledge the presence of a superior rationality behind the existence of the universe as it is to comprehend a theologian who would deny the advances of science."[10]

Truly, we can now say that the testimonies of the cosmological and teleological witnesses of God are indeed glorious, as they greatly magnify our Creator and reveal the wonder of what this mysterious God truly is capable of.

A Summary of Our Observational and Logical Conclusions So Far

In reviewing the information that we have covered so far, what can be reasonably implied from our understanding pertaining to the miracle of life?

1) *There must have been a decisive, personal initiative in creating the universe at some point in the past.*

Life originating from blind chance or random natural processes is not a plausible explanation for the creation. The probabilities that we reviewed render naturalism as irrational, pointing instead to the existence of an Intelligent Mind. If there ever was a time when nothing existed, then nothing would currently exist. Nothingness has no energy to create or produce anything. But since the universe was nothing at one moment, and in the next moment everything appeared, a source of power that was *decisively exercised from a decision-making Mind* must have existed. This mind that produced this universe is what we refer to as God.

If God were merely a blind impersonal law or "higher power" such as energy or a force (i.e. Mother Nature, Brahman, karma, etc.) as some religions might claim, then we would still expect nothing to exist right now.

Non-personal natural forces simply exist in a state of indifference without creative ability or initiative. A force cannot creatively bring about the perfect constants that facilitate orderly and conscious life, especially anything more complex than itself—such as living, rational, and conscious beings.

2) *We can know that God is a necessary and eternally self-existent immaterial Being.*

We can reasonably conclude that God is eternal and self-existent free from any physical substance. The contents of the universe are dependent upon His very existence, which makes God alone the single necessary precondition for not just biological life but also all material and chemical reality too. We owe the experience of existence and our ability to ponder things to the One in whom all knowledge originated.

Since God as a necessary Being must exist, *it is logically impossible for atheism to be true*; since atheism isn't true, godless religions and worldviews must also be false. This includes atheistic tenants that are found in Buddhism, Jainism, Hinduism, Confucianism, and certain Pagan and Wiccan traditions as well. The foundations of these worldviews praise creatures or the material world rather than the Creator.

3) *We know that God is all-powerful with the capability of producing miracles.*

Any Being capable of creating our natural world out of nothing can safely be considered all-powerful. God can literally bring about what previously "is not" into existence, putting a form to "what is." He is the painter that literally creates His canvas, paints, frame, and brush, along with the beautiful artwork. He is a supernatural, miracle-working God.

This implies that we live in a world where the miraculous is indeed possible and can be expected to take place by the permissive power of God in time and space.

Consequently, miracles contained in the Bible such as the prophet Jonah surviving three days in the stomach of a great fish, the waves of the Red Sea parting to provide dry land for people to walk across, the ability to walk on water, people surviving otherwise fatal accidents, or a person being resurrected from the dead are all mere child's play to a Being of this magnitude. He may overrule or suspend any of *His* natural laws for *His* divine prerogatives whenever He chooses to do so. The belief in supernatural miracles in a universe governed by such a Being is therefore a completely rational viewpoint.

4) *We know indirectly that there can only be one necessary God.*

In the cosmological witness, we have seen that there can be only one God. Having two or more necessary Beings would be a logical contradiction, since only one necessary source can be the required framework for all contingencies. To be defined as necessary is to stand alone on a higher plane than all other things. Two necessary gods could never initiate the first decisive cause that sparked the beginning of the universe. Only one Being could ever truly reserve this name for Himself and be the source for all other created beings. At best, we might say that there could be other contingent spiritual beings (such as angels) created by God; but they are not the same essence as the one truly necessary God. There can only be one all-powerful, all-knowing God—one divine "I AM."

If God is one in essence, then all other religions that promote the idea of numerous necessary gods or creator gods of equal power must be considered false.

Where Do We Go from Here?

I trust that, by now, your pursuit of a personal God has been rationally quickened. Let us continue on with this presupposition in place—that a personal God must exist first *before* an orderly world ever could.

Going forward, let us see if we can find out any other information that might lead us to understand who this God might be. Does He have recognizable morals or personal attributes like us? We have used clues in the natural world to show us what exactly God "is"—now let's continue to find out who this God is through the natural world of human nature.

3

Moral Demonstrations
OF GOD'S GLORY

One of the places where we can understand the personal nature of God without direct personal revelation is by looking at something that essentially governs human activity—the characteristics of morality.

Mankind has an instinctual awareness of what is right and wrong. This is where ethics and morals come into play. Morals and ethics are linked, but are not the same thing. Ethics is the moral ideal or could be called *absolute moral truth*. Ethics attempts to wrestle with what a perfect moral judgment would look like in any situation. One could see ethics as a detailed look into how we—in a perfect world—*ought* to morally govern ourselves. Ethics are objective in this sense, binding our consciences to the knowledge of a higher absolute moral standard.

Morals, on the other hand, are the patterns of behavior found in a person or a group of people in their ethical discovery. The morals of certain cultures and individuals change time and time again. This often depends upon the influential waves of thinking going on at the societal level. In other words, ethics are external absolutes, and morals are internal drives toward ethical truth. In this way, something could be said to be both *morally right* in accordance to a society, yet e*thically wrong* at the same time; for simplicity's sake, I will focus mainly on morality, since this internal drive for ethical truth is another clear fingerprint of God.

Morality

All people feel an inescapable value that is placed upon the various aspects of honesty, respect, fairness, love, integrity, goodness, and justice. We know that a certain choice is the "right thing to do" at a given time, even if we sometimes can't fully explain how or why we might know this to be true. This is what we would call our conscience.

Not only do we positively know these virtues to be right and good, but we also experience it negatively as well. For instance, when we commit abuses against others, our conscience judges us with the sting of moral failure. Guilt, regret, PTSD, remorse, disappointment, and even depression are ways in which we are haunted from encounters with moral failure. They haunt us because, morally, we know what others (or we) should have done—but because of certain circumstances, fell short of it. These encounters of moral failure in the end birth trauma or disturb us so greatly as to affect our life both consciously and subconsciously.

Ethics and Morality Rationally Point to God

The drive for what is right is an unseen tool that provides a unique basis for being human. Some who might have certain disabilities or disorders can be severely lacking in moral judgment, but aside from those exceptions to the rule, the mentally stable and healthy individual possesses this tool in order to govern personal and communal relationships. It even influences our reasonability and rationality, bringing our thinking into abstract moral categories of thought, further distinguishing us from the animal kingdom. Morals are a wonderful blessing that, when used properly, enable us to maintain civil relationships, feel love, express emotion, seek desire, reason properly, and experience deeply the pleasure of being human.

The moment we begin to reflect upon how we ought to treat one another, or how we ought to be treated by others, we are in fact looking outside of ourselves, into the realm of absolutes, in order to find the ethical answer. We are assuming the answer is objectively outside of us. We know the answer is "out there," even if we don't know exactly where to look or agree on how to achieve it. In this way, we are appealing to an absolute standard of law—a truth fixed and preserved within a personally existing Moral Law Giver.

Since we have seen that all physical things, such as constants and living organisms, have been carefully created and precisely arranged in purposeful order, we must ask the question—why wouldn't non-physical truths like morals also have a designed purpose? Most importantly, what does this say about God?

It seems unreasonable to think that God would create something as universally-binding as moral intuition without the intention of us putting it into use. It seems that when our Creator developed humans, He did so with an access point to moral absolutes (ethics) that exist in Him. Why else would inner guiding principles exist if not for the benefit of personal relationships? What other purpose would it serve? Moral nature can only be based reasonably out of a God who is very concerned with the moral judgments in His chief creation: man.

On Naturalism and Morals

Morals must be divine because naturalism cannot sufficiently explain ethical truths and morals without God. Some naturalists say that morality is an evolutionary, interactive device to aid survival. Others say that moral truth is dependent upon a person's personal opinions or preferences, which carries us back to the claim of relativism, with its own problems that we saw earlier. In this view, morals are subjective—dependent upon our emotional opinion.

The claim that there are no moral absolutes implies that what is right for one person is not necessarily right for another. For one person, lying on a resume or cheating on a test might be perfectly acceptable in order to advance their career, while another person might condone stealing if it proves beneficial to them in the long run. This view assumes that morals are based on the arbitrary ruling of personal choice. If this were true, then all societies with justice systems are inconsistent. If no moral absolutes exist, then criminal activity doesn't truly exist. Legal codes (which assume moral absolutes) could never be a standard bound to anyone consistently. Under this view, the behavior of a criminal is more of an alternate lifestyle.

This view is popular today and seems attractive to many—that is, until the person is personally cheated, stolen from, or impacted by a murder in their immediate family. At that point, opinions quickly shift from the thought that morals are subjective to the acknowledgement that they have been objectively wronged, and the guilty culprit must be brought to justice. At least, that is how they would act. All the while, this would be inconsistent with their belief. Relativism cannot be rationally lived out or consistently held; therefore, this worldview is self-defeating, disqualifying it from being a reasonable view of reality.

Evolutionary Naturalism

If we add evolutionary naturalism into the mix, many other problematic issues arise. If we are simply evolved, ape-like mammals, as atheistic naturalism presupposes, then we are nothing more than sophisticated animals—animals that cannot be blamed for the biological instincts that we possess. Our chemical makeup has already been predetermined according to naturalism, and now all we can do is just go with the genetic flow.

Morally repugnant instincts that we see in humans, such as infanticide, rape, gang warfare, and kidnapping are actually fairly common and widespread in the animal world—even the primate world. Since it is considered to be *natural* for animals to act upon these desires, why is it that we can't follow these same animalistic instincts?

Some might suggest that primitive behaviors are not advantageous for us in a civil society. The person who argues this is making the assumption that civility is the moral ideal, but this is actually what needs to be explained. Furthermore, if moral civility is being considered beneficial or advantageous, then the question arises: what does society define as advantageous? Advantageous in a world of evolved monkeys is arbitrary; in fact, one could counter-argue that to oppress others could prove to be very advantageous for a civil society.

Some might respond that a culture is best to determine its own morality. What is right for some people might not be right for others. For instance, my resident country of Canada determines what is right in Canada, Mexico determines what is right in Mexico and so on. This still does not escape an arbitrary standard of determining right from wrong. Which political leader or party ought to have the final say in accepting what will be considered ethically-binding for all in a country? One dilemma is that an entire nation can be morally bankrupt and therefore not wise in many cases to allow the moral position of a society to declare their "own morality," especially if that position is an unethical one. What political figure, philosopher, or religious leader could ever rightfully subject an entire population of mixed ethical and religious beliefs to submit to the mere moral opinion of a few... and then make it law. Cultural moralism breaks down, because it ultimately rests upon one or a group of individuals making the rules for everyone, which is an arbitrary law.

To put it in a more sobering way, couldn't it be argued (if we are, in fact, just animals) that rape and murder are actually not truly crimes but alternative lifestyles with the goal of passing on genes? Murder kills off competitors, while technically, civility can be known to obstruct reproduction by increasing tolerance among other males that are in competition with one another. In this way, murder could aid the dominant males in sexual reproduction.

Forcing a young woman to submit for breeding purposes in order to carry along the male's seed seems consistent with the structure of some mammalian herds. Waiting for the socially appropriate spousal commitments can become a disadvantage if rape uses the time and energy of a male more efficiently. Forgive the graphic nature of my points, but if the naturalist worldview is a good worldview to follow, we must be consistent with accepting the logical and moral conclusions as well.

Think of it this way—we don't get mad at a male lion for acting upon his instinct to attack and kill another male lion, if necessary, in order to establish dominance over a pride. By killing the previous male's cubs, the new conquering male lion brings the lionesses into heat sooner, which allows him to produce his own offspring faster, thus preserving his genetic survival. Since actions of violence are instinctual for mammals for this purpose, why oppose gang warfare, which could be considered a different rendition of the same territorial and sexual instincts? Isn't gang warfare an equivalent human action, parallel to the instincts of apes or chimpanzee groups in the wild? How can one evolved ape insist that another evolved ape conform to *his personal choice* of societal laws, especially when it opposes the "survival of the fittest" instinct that evolution defends?

Genghis Khan would be the poster boy for consistent evolutionary belief (if he would have held that view). Genghis slaughtered potential competition and raped his way through Asia, impregnating innumerable women, giving birth to countless children—so much so that his reign contributed to a great population increase throughout the centuries in Asia, as generations continued on. Many people in the Asian world today can actually attribute their existence to the immoral actions of this man. Genghis Khan was an incredible success story, as far as evolution is concerned. Why should we not also consistently march to the beat of his drum if evolution is true?

Ethics that Fight Against Evolution

A case could also be made that *our inner drive toward ethical truth opposes the selfishness required by evolutionism to be successful.* Moral drive seems to be an annoyingly counter-intuitive characteristic from an evolutionary perspective. The building of hospitals and healthcare centers seem to be widely recognized as a good thing, and yet, in our attempt to preserve these institutions, we are housing those who, according to evolutionary theory, are considered to be weak and unfit for survival. Do we delay the natural advancement of the human race by having these facilities that prevent evolution from speeding things along? I don't see how an evolutionist can logically avoid this implication. The ethical truths that lead our consciences to begin such loving institutions in the first place are the very truths that caused us to ignore the moral implications of evolution theory. Praise God for that!

One other such example of a moral drive that opposes itself against evolution is altruism. Altruism could be expressed as a self-sacrificial devotion to the welfare of others. Many forms of altruism are acts of love toward the diseased, disabled, weak, elderly, poor, dying, and others who are exposed to many other levels of disadvantage. Self-sacrifice is counterintuitive to an animalistic drive toward the self-preservation claimed by evolutionary theory. Rather than eliminating competition, it actively seeks to preserve those who are selected naturally for death, according to the processes of evolution.

It is interesting to reflect upon the fact that this type of love is esteemed as the highest virtue in many cultures. When we hear of selfless acts performed for strangers, our hearts leap in joyful celebration, often being moved to tears at such acts of selfless love. Why is this?

I submit to you that we are emotionally-charged by these acts because they represent the ultimate picture of purity in love that all long for and desire to be a part of. These feelings and emotions are not given to us in vain—they direct us and alert our consciences toward a rightful view of peace, love, and mercy, all of which sit comfortably with us as the image bearers of God.

What if There Were no Absolute Morals?

If moral absolutes don't actually exist—as the naturalistic worldview would imply—then we would have to withhold all forms of moral judgment. To be consistent, we would be required to tolerate all forms of moral expression. The atheistic world is a relative world and, in that relative world, there is no good nor bad, right nor wrong—just a difference of opinion.

The terrorist kills because it seems right to him, according to his worldview—in his mind, he is fighting for a bigger moral picture or the greater good. In fact, it could be successfully argued that all evil actions are done for some type of grand moral picture—at least in the mind of the person doing the act. It is in the dark world of relativism that acts of evil become justifiable.

JEFF MCCONNELL

Politician A might slander and publish lies against Politician B in an effort to sway the vote of the people. In the end, Politician A may feel that the lie was justified for the "greater good." It was done to prevent people from stepping into a dangerous opposing political idea—dangerous, at least, in Politician A's mind.

If it is true that all views are relative, then why seek to change another's mind or tell him he that he is wrong? Who are we to judge Muslim extremists? Who are we to judge the ideas of the Nazis' actions in the concentration camps as immoral? If there is no absolute moral standard *beyond* mankind, then there is no objective standard *within* mankind either. Morals are bankrupt and powerless. In this view, Hitler is not morally worse off than Mother Teresa—they just differ in their preferences on how to treat others. Hitler's decision to murder Jews for the good of a race is just as valuable as cradling dying children in love—motives are technically useless to ethics if atheistic naturalism is true.

Luckily, those who believe in atheistic naturalism or relativism are not living in a consistent manner. If they were acting consistently, then culturally, we would be in huge trouble. If you were to indoctrinate such a worldview into the minds of impressionable children and raise them upon these ideas consistently, then you would produce a society of sociopathic adults with complete disregard for others.

Thankfully, when it comes to education, naturalistic parents instinctually teach their children what is right and wrong, in spite of their views. They still live, to some degree, as though ethics are morally-binding on everyone. They generally attempt to treat others as they would want to be treated, and by doing this, they show clear evidence that the objective golden rule has been impressed upon their soul by their Creator.

Cross-Cultural Morals

The phenomenon of cross-cultural morality produces a strong and reasonable case in the question of moral truth. There has been no known human culture without some sort of societal standard for justice in order to hold others accountable for bad behavior.

In every country, criminal behavior is seen as an ethical problem that must be addressed and corrected through some sort of justice system. Though the penalties and legal procedures may differ, they are all unified in their attempt to strive for the promotion of what is right and just. Their codes of justice seek to deal with ethical problems such as murder, theft, adultery, dishonesty, etc. One society may cut off the hand of a thief as punishment, while another might force the thief to pay a small fine. Regardless of the penalty given, both cultures are clearly aware of the violation of the moral principle—do not steal—and are attempting to bring justice to the victim.

As I stated earlier, if you cannot live out the logical implications of your worldview (such as relativism), then it fails to properly account for the moral reality that we are a part of. God alone can best explain our drive for morality and justice.

The God of Ethics

The only reasonable explanation for our moral pull toward ethics is that God has provided for us an inner template for moral guidance. This template was originally found in His person, which is reflective of His perfectly moral nature. In this way, those who believe in a personal God have the most reasonable explanation as to why people ought to be treated with dignity and respect. Humans are valuable because God has created them with a greater uniqueness than the animals, which gives humans that higher creative value we all recognize. With this in mind, those who believe in a personal God can alone provide a livable and consistent foundation for living in mutual dignity and respect with fellow human beings.

Those who believe in God can consistently welcome moral reformers that relativism ought to ignore and discourage. Reformers such as William Wilberforce, Martin Luther King, and Mother Teresa, who in their writings and actions have overturned many blind spots of evil in their day, are considered to be generally moral in their lives. They believed that the morals of society are not relative but that evils must be overturned so we might seek to obey the moral absolute of love that has been given to us by God. They believed that true morality ought to behave in a certain way. Those who deny the existence of God, however, cannot consistently defend ethics or advocate for human rights, since by doing so, they are doing the very thing that they deny exists—defending a universal moral right. This is a hopelessly self-defeating worldview.

As we have stated already, naturalism is every society's worst moral nightmare. This view can be used as a helpful tool for anyone who wishes to justify following through with the evil desires of their heart, paving the way for moral chaos and unbridled anarchy. In the theoretical world of consistent naturalism, physical laws are all that there truly is, so whatever aids you in the survival of yourself is ultimately the only "ethic"—kill or be killed; survival depends upon this. This worldview equates humans to mere chemicals, gases, and distant relatives of stardust. The value of human life quickly crumbles under such claims. Logically, rationally, and practically speaking, relativism is not an accurate reflection of reality.

In contrast, God has designed us with an inner guide to let us know when we have gone too far. There is a right and wrong to be objectively found in the mind of a personal God and we all have inner access to that reality through our conscience. If moral absolutes exist, then so does God, our Law Giver.

4
Personal Demonstrations
OF GOD'S GLORY

What science tells us about the mind points strongly towards some version or other of physicalism. The intuitions, in one way or another, suggest that there is something seriously incomplete about any purely physical story about the mind...

FRANK JACKSON (AUSTRALIAN ANALYTIC PHILOSOPHER)

then the LORD God formed the man of dust from the ground and breathed into his nostrils the breath of life, and the man became a living creature.

GENESIS 2:7

Another area in the natural world where the personality of God is made clearly visible is implied within the mystery of our own personal nature. Our inner personhood is a vastly complex part of who we are. Our personality contains various types of non-material characteristics, such as emotions, intentions, character, intelligence, creativity, habits, hopes, intuition, worldviews, and dreams. It distinguishes who we are apart from other people in a way far beyond the explanations of the natural world. Your personhood is *non-material* in nature, and yet it still exists. Our personality has no satisfactory naturalistic explanation.

In a materialistic universe, how could simple matter ever form a personal consciousness that ponders abstract thoughts? Our physical bodies literally exist in a continuous state of change and renewal. Trillions of microscopic cells work around the clock, replacing the older, weaker, and dying cells. In fact, every two years, new replicated cells will replace every old cell in your body. In this way, you essentially become a new physical person, coded afresh through the instruction and information manuals located in your own specialized DNA. And yet, oddly enough, who you are remains largely unaffected through that bodily replacement: your memories, personality, habits, preferences, and morals continue to carry over the years and decades as your body continuously replaces itself over and over again. It's a bit like replacing computer hardware (physical components) piece by piece while the software (immaterial components such as documents, files, and information) remains intact throughout the entire transition!

As we continue to mature and grow, the entity of our personhood remains the same—or at least similar—year after year. *This continuous self-consciousness is what mankind traditionally refers to as a soul or spirit.* Since we have an immaterial soul equipped with self-consciousness, consciousness, memories, and personhood, it is reasonable for us to conclude that this "software" is a central part of our non-physical design.

Isn't it interesting that our bodies have a sort of ghost-in-the-machine type of assembly? The luxury car is physically laid out for the benefit and convenience of the driver inside; so too our bodies are assembled around the central intelligence of our soul, which runs the controls. The body might be rightly identified as a near perfect vehicle for the soul, made complete with easily maneuverable hands, feet, eyes, and ears serving the commands made by the central consciousness that is YOU. Once the driver (the non-physical soul) leaves, the car (physical body) ceases to function according to its purpose and rusts away. There is an interesting dichotomy that exists in the human being: one that is material and another that is immaterial, staying in place even when the physical body is completely replaced. After reflecting upon these truths, the concept of life after death is actually a very reasonable natural assumption that many people have.

Man's Appreciation and Recognition of Beauty

Northern lights, glowing phosphorus creatures of Earth, and the birth of a baby—all these things contain inspired elements of beauty and wonder. We are strangely drawn to those delightfully memorable moments where we come face to face with breathtaking beauty.

The loveliness of life possesses the power to change our personality. Beauty is the leading source of artistic inspiration in a culture. Poetry and prose deal with the beauty of language. Music deals with the lust for a melodious tune—all of these things are a form of artistic human expression based upon something beautiful.

Our attraction to beauty is an otherworldly experience. This appeal provides for us this important point to ponder: why is it that people are happy when experiencing beauty? Why is it that we can experience wonderful things and feel this deep sense of awe? This feeling is not only foundational for artistic expression, but ultimately leads us to ask the question: why is it there in the first place? Where is this deep-rooted sense ultimately found, if not in the careful design of our Creator—the Author of beauty itself?

As we have seen already, God has created and designed all physical things with an intended purpose in mind—this even includes non-physical things such as our affection toward beautiful things. The emotions that we feel toward beauty would not be so consistently spread across the hearts of all cultures unless God had purposed it to be so.

Naturalism cannot account for personal experiences with natural beauty (the sense of awe) nor explain with any satisfaction any evolutionary advantage behind the emotions associated with it. Beauty is often embraced in periods of intimate self-reflection and seems to offer nothing practical to the desire of reproduction—it looks to be more of a distraction, if anything.

In a worldview with God as the centerpiece, this desire makes a world of sense. Because we are creatures made in the likeness of God and not evolutionary machines, we benefit from extra features that enable life to be the great stimulating adventure that it is. We are more than stardust—we are created by God to do great things and embrace the little beauties in life that we commonly take for granted. If the Lord is able to grant us these gifts in a world stained by evil, then surely the religious longing for a beautiful utopian paradise is rationally supported. Concepts of Heaven are therefore reasonable too, and would be desirable if it were revealed by God that there was truth to such a place.

Our Dependency upon Logic

To reason effectively and think clearly, we must obey certain basic principles of coherent thought—these laws of coherency are what we call the laws of logic. These laws are not subjective inventions of the mind, but rather universal and cross-cultural laws naturally acted upon without second thought. As we stated earlier, objective immaterial truths are always true, even if no one is around to observe them—this is what makes them objective. They have no substance; they "exist" beyond the material world. These laws of thought are necessary to the thinking process—by which we come to understand anything in the world.

We are programmed by God to function with these first principles of logic, since to be without them, all thinking, communication, language, or understanding would be impossible. Two of the most basic axioms of logic are the *law of non-contradiction*, and *the law of the excluded middle.*

The law of non-contradiction states that *something cannot be one thing and its opposite at the same time and in the same way.* The sun cannot be shining and not shining at the same time in the same way. A dog cannot be a dog and not a dog, for if this is believed, it is then a contradiction—the law of non-contradiction reveals to us this truth. This is Basic Thinking 101.

The law of the excluded middle says that *something must either be or not be.* There isn't any middle option or third possibility. Your television is either on or off; there is no in between. A thing either *is* or *is not.*

In short, these first principles of thought give us a natural ability to know the difference between statements that are logically sound or contradictory. As we investigate the world for truth, these mental tools make black and white clarity possible on many issues, including mathematical formulas and abstract concepts. Without these two rules of logic (and many others), we could never really acknowledge anything to be true. Logic is thus essential for us in determining certainty about anything.

Even observational science is *conditioned upon the consistency of logical interpretation*—without logic, science and mathematics are dead disciplines. We can calculate forces behind an object in physics or troubleshoot chemical reactions properly only in accordance with logical and rational understandings.

Even personal experiences are only understood through the lens of these eternal, non-changing, objective laws of thought. When we experience a rock, our senses of touch and sight reflect certain impressions upon our mind, which in turn provides us with knowledge about the rock (i.e. the surface of the rock is hard, not soft). If we were to examine an apple, the senses with which we experience the apple would enable us to understand the distinct, undeniable truths about that fruit, such as its wonderful taste. After experiencing both the rock and the apple with our senses, we can properly discern and describe their differences with the laws of logic.

Immaterial and eternal truths such as logic, ethics, and mathematics could not arise from anything physical, since they themselves are immaterial concepts accessible through the rational mind alone. You cannot *touch* ethical values, you cannot *taste* mathematical laws, and you cannot *see* the laws of logic, yet these things are foundational before you even begin to think.

Where Naturalism and Evolution Fail Logic

If there is no such thing as absolute immaterial truths, then logic and our ability to reason are not fixed, and our mind can't be trusted. Our ability to reason is likely only the current thinking pattern that has developed at this point in our stage of evolution. The mind evolves, according to the evolutionist, so the thinking mind would be in constant change also. If this were true, we could never settle on any rational train of thought or the experience of the senses that informs our mind.

At best, these laws (like morals) would be delusions, relative to each person's electro-chemical brain processes. Someone who has more chemical fizzing going on in their brain might be able to reason better than someone who has less brain-fizzing. If that's the case, then we have no reason to trust any mind, because all thoughts may soon evolve to accept that it is perfectly rational to believe in contradictions! Maybe two plus two will one day equal seventeen. Some people would see a car and a human as identical objects. If the worldview of naturalism is true, we have no objective ground to reason from. How could anyone ever put their trust in changing electro-chemical reactions to tell us what is true? We can only imagine what kind of rational chaos this would produce.

If the chemical reactions of the brain are always changing their processes, then our ideas about the standard for truth would obviously change too. Christian philosopher Ronald Nash sums up the atheist's problem well: "Naturalism's major problem, then, is explaining how mindless forces give rise to minds, knowledge, and sound reasoning. But every naturalist wants others to think that his Naturalism is a consequence of his sound reasoning."[11] In this sense, naturalism is a self-destructive and self-defeating worldview.

God Explains Logic and Reason

Thankfully, with God as our center for objective reality, we can know that the immaterial logical truths of the mind that we notice are, in fact, there. Two plus two will always equal four in all possible worlds, and there will always be immaterial laws of logic found in the thinking mind, because without them, no thinking can ever be done. Without logic, no thinking mind can exist.

The skeptics must realize that every question ever asked, every answer given, every statement made, every thought pondered presupposes the existence of a personal God. The skeptic thinks to himself, "Where is the evidence for God?" But if you look carefully, this simple question is loaded with objective assumptions. For example, the question itself is communicated using the assumed *laws of logic*, and is concerned with asking a *moral* question concerning what is *rationally true*. These things—*logic, morals, and rational truth*—have a *basis, not in naturalism, but through the existence of God.* Even though atheists live in denial of God, they must communicate and reason as though God *already* exists in order to make any meaningful, ethical, or rational statements. The theist alone possesses a truly consistent view of reality—a reality that must presuppose God to explain the reason for thought in the first place.

A Summary of Conclusions about Who God Is

1) *Since morals, personhood, and logic are a part of our creation, it seems reasonable to conclude that God is likewise concerned with morals, personhood, and clear thinking.*

   From the vast cosmos to the hidden world of micro-machines, God is purposeful in His work. If indeed *purposeful*, then a reason for it must lay somewhere beyond it in the rational mind of God. Ethical drives, consciousness, attraction to beauty, and logical thoughts are clues testifying to who God is. The key to understanding why God would create us with these immaterial attributes seems to be found in their effects. These things provide us a beneficial understanding of the world, help us establish relationships with others, and suggest His glory—they are likely created for this end.

No artist, engineer, or architect creates anything without purpose or intent—we should expect the same. God wants us to live with moral accountability and sound thinking in our minds—He wants us to be reasonable creatures. In the worldview of the theist, we are not chemical versions of stardust but possess purposefulness and a value made obvious through the creation.

2) God creates personality, and therefore, this further supports a supernatural Personal Being.

At one time, God was the only thing existing, until the world came into being by His hand. In order to create this world, God had to have first existed independent of the natural world. It is from this place God made the decision to willfully initiate an orderly physical universe. This initiative or decision to begin this work and to maintain its order could only be decided upon by the choice of a rational thinking mind—a mind with personal attributes. Thus, God is a rational and personal God.

A relational understanding of God eliminates all the impersonal depictions of God in the worldviews of many world religions, such as in Pantheism (the view that everything is God) and Panentheism (the view that God is the soul of both the universe and beyond the physical world). Both of these understandings of God exist in religions such as Hinduism, Taoism, and some forms of tribal Animism. We must follow where the reason takes us, and in this case, it takes us far away from some of the most widespread religious views that are popularized in Western culture.

Where Do We Go from Here?

So far, we have looked at the natural world with many different emphases, revealing the awesome fingerprints of an all-powerful, necessary, and eternally personal God. We learned that He alone is self-existent and demonstrated His power by initiating the physical universe. This also led us to the existence of moral and rational-thinking creatures.

We have now come to the end of natural revelation's ability to teach us who God is. While we were able to clearly understand some things about God through the process of examining the natural world, this natural knowledge only took us so far. At this point in our investigation, we are left bound to our natural limitations, unable to proceed any further in figuring out who God is.

At this point, questions still remain to be answered. Is God directly involved in His creation or is He indifferent toward us altogether? He could have created all things at one point in time but is now absent from us, working on new projects elsewhere in the universe, leaving us to the care of His pitiless natural law. Is one of these possibilities the case?

Let us now conclude our observations of the natural and see if a different source of information might exist that could potentially broaden our insight in understanding who God is. The question now is—has God revealed Himself in any other special way? Has God ever spoken to us in a different, more communicative way?

Could you imagine the value of having received direct contact from our divine Creator? The written message of our Creator could potentially reveal the secrets and answers to many of life's innermost mysteries. Why is the world here? What is God like? Why is there evil and suffering? What does God desire of us? What happens after we die? The value of this information could put to bed centuries of philosophical speculation, religious dogma, political disputes, and scientific assumptions. This information would be the most important information for the human race to know.

Any message of divine authority that God gives would become the chief standard by which we can judge all assumptions and ideas. If God revealed truth to us, then this truth (God's truth) would be the best possible worldview and logically render all contradictory opinion and opposing systems of belief false. For instance, if God said that there is indeed life after death, then atheism and religious ideas of annihilation after death would be naturally removed from the smorgasbord of possible worldview choices. It is this question that we will focus on for the remainder of this book. Has God revealed Himself to us, and if he has, what did He have to say?

Section 2

SPECIAL REVELATION

5

Has God Revealed Himself
ANOTHER WAY?

The major religions on the Earth contradict each other left and right. You can't all be correct. And what if all of you are wrong? It's a possibility, you know. You must care about the truth, right? Well, the way to winnow through all the differing contentions is to be skeptical.

CARL SAGAN, CONTACT

...We ought not to think that the divine being is like gold or silver or stone, an image formed by the art and imagination of man. The times of ignorance God overlooked, but now he commands all people everywhere to repent.

ACTS 17:29-30

Even if you have accepted the reality of God, another problem still remains. Who is this God? Out of all the gods found in the different religions, which God is the true one? Could it be that there is no religion that best represents Him? The problem is that different religions and worldviews have conflicting beliefs about who God is. They can't all be right, so which one carries the true view? This issue of "which God

95

should we worship" is a problem that we must face next as we continue in our quest for the knowledge of the One True Living God.

Before we continue, let me first deliver a solemn warning to all readers, including myself. As human beings, we must be reminded that we have a strong tendency to psychologically create what we want to hear when it comes to spiritual things. We do this when we invent for ourselves a god to suit our own divine preferences—this invention of a god is called *idolatry*.

The temptation is to believe in only the "positive" and comforting aspects of God. Some choose to believe that God is strictly loving, some prefer forever patient, still others view God as the endless giver of second chances, using material blessings to provide everyone with a nice, cozy existence on Earth.

By letting our subjective feelings govern our reason, our views of God will then become murky, at best. On top of that, we also bring to the plate our own emotional and experiential-based filters, which further cloud our already limited view of God.

The truth seeker must not be persuaded by superstition, politics, or popular religion. Instead, our great pleasure in life is to be wholly committed to the adventure of seeking after God as best we can. Blind faith has no role in the quest for truth; instead, we must seek sensible conclusions based upon solid evidence, which paves a rational path toward the True God.

At this point, our knowledge admittedly tells us very little about the character of God, so we must cautiously avoid ascribing character qualities to God yet. This discussion will be explored in further chapters.

Has God Ever Communicated to Man?

Has the personal God of the universe ever attempted to communicate to mankind? If God created logic, reason, morality, and knowledge, then surely it follows that communicating to us wouldn't be a challenge for Him. God is, after all, the inventor of language, communication, and understanding. *Has God ever allowed Himself to be sought out, or has He ever taken the initiative to reveal Himself to men?*

If God had chosen *not* to be known, then the worldview of *deism* would be the correct worldview to embrace. In deism, all that we have discovered about God would be our limit. Apart from philosophical ponderings, nothing of real substance would ultimately be added to help us understand the Creator—just our mere speculation. In essence, deism embraces understanding that God created all things (for reasons unknown except for Himself) and has left the universe alone to govern itself according to His natural laws that He set in place.

Deism holds to the view that evidence for God is forcefully compelling but denies that God had ever communicated to man. There is no supernatural revelation, no scriptures, no prophecies, no visions, nothing expressed through language. However, if it could be known that God *has* indeed spoken to mankind, then the worldview of deism falls flat on its face.

Hypothetically speaking, let's say that God *did* contact us—how could we tell if the message was truly of God? How could we know that the message is not some man-made religion or mystical babblings from a charismatic false prophet or cult leader? What kind of "fingerprint" from God could we rationally expect as being a part of His divine message?

I think two main criteria would be sufficient.

1) *The message itself would announce the claim of divine inspiration.*

God could speak in a variety of different ways and through many different means. He could communicate through an audible voice from the heavens, through visions or dreams, or some type of written account in any language. God could also speak through a group of people, a race, a country—maybe through a lone prophetic messenger or a group of ambassadors sent to the world to passionately herald the oracles of God.

Regardless of how God chooses to proclaim His message, it is reasonably certain that the message would make the claim that it contains divine authority or inspiration. If God would desire us to know Him, He would need to announce to us that it is Him communicating, so that we might have a way of distinguishing His message from others. Otherwise, how could He expect us to acknowledge the message as His? Just as we sign our name to a written letter or email to communicate the origin as belonging to us, likewise, God would need to convey that the message He provides is directly sanctioned by Him—a "thus sayeth the Lord" type of acknowledgment.

If that oracle does confess to have been originated from God, then we ought to seek the authenticity of that claim by using the next criterion.

2) *The message would contain a miraculous mark of divine communication.*

In order to differentiate whether a message is from man or God, some form of supernatural authentication is a logical expectation—a verifying mark that this message is unique. Nothing will grab the attention of rational beings like something unexplainable or miraculous. God is capable of miraculous work, and if He were to authenticate His message, then we ought to expect the miraculous to surround that authentication from God as a way of showing us unmistakably that it is His.

Many religious messages have been qualified with the first criteria (the claim of authority from God), but something more is needed. We must not be foolish enough to assume that just because something is claimed to be divine that it actually is. Without any additional proof, we are justified in our skepticism because we must be able to tell the difference between true and false religion by more than just what the message proclaims about itself. The only way that we can see a message as having divine influence or authorship is if the miraculous confirmed the divine authority of that message.

Which Religions Would Qualify?

Since many of the Eastern religions and spiritualties, such as Hinduism and Taoism, are either atheistic or believe in a person-less God or "power," then we can easily conclude (from the law of non-contradiction) that these religions would be false at their foundation. Which religions in the world would claim to have both the qualifications of divine inspiration in a personal God and claim miraculous signs?

Strangely (and thankfully), there have been only a handful of religions that have actually held to a monotheistic personal God that claimed to possess a special proclamation of God's revelation. While numerous sects and cults have claimed these elements, the strongest and most convincing of these religions comes down to either the religion of Islam or Judaism and Christianity. First, we will reflect upon the religious system of Islam to see if there are any satisfactory grounds for the inspiration that they claim to possess.

The Quran

Criterion 1: The message itself would announce the claim of divine inspiration.

According to Islam, God chose to reveal Himself to the prophet Muhammad through the angel Gabriel in a series of messages. These revelations that were given to Muhammad in a cave were then written down in the Arabic language, in what would come to be known as the Quran—the book that Muslims believe to be divinely inspired.

The Quran (or recitations) claim to be divinely inspired, without straying, and in proper guidance according to the divine desire of God:

Surah 53:2-4 is speaking of Muhammad when it says, "...your companion has neither strayed nor is he misguided, nor does he speak out of his own desire."[12]

Islam therefore fits the first criterion, claiming to be a revelation inspired by God through the Arabic language. This criterion is a reasonable claim in our first of the two qualifiers for divine inspiration. But will it hold as firmly as we observe the second of the qualifiers?

Criterion 2: The message would contain a miraculous mark of divine communication.

There are scriptures in the Quran that imply our second criterion, stating that miracles can be seen as a clear confirmation

100

of God's word. Sura 23:44-46 describes this with Moses' sign as a clear authority:

"Then We sent Our Messengers in succession. Whenever a Messenger came to his people they rejected him, calling him a liar. Thereupon, We made each people to follow the other (to its doom), reducing them to mere tales (of the past). Scourged be the people who do not believe! *Then We sent Moses and his brother Aaron with Our Signs and a clear authority to Pharaoh and to his chiefs,* but they behaved superciliously and they were haughty."

This scripture leads us to believe that Moses and Aaron as messengers of God were sent with signs and a clear authority of God. God worked miraculously through them, and so this ought to have been evident to the people God was saving. Here, the Quran states the clear importance of the miraculous signs in their vindication of divine authority.

What About Muhammad's Miracles?

So what does the Quran show us in regard to the miraculous confirmations of Muhammad as a prophet of God?

Out of the few apparent miracles in the Quran, such as Muhammad's night journey, the Victory at Badar, or the splitting of Muhammad's breast, even the Quran doesn't outright attest to these events as being miraculous. Assuming that these indeed were indeed miraculous, there is still the problem of having no historical evidence to verify or confirm their authenticity.

Most miracles that are reported to have been from Muhammad are written in the Hadith, which is a Muslim religious book, though not considered by many Muslims to be inspired by God. The miraculous claims that were presented in the Hadith were recorded 100-200 years after the death of Muhammad and his original followers, which provides enough time for legend to sweep in and embellish the original events. These miracles also seem to contradict Muhammad's own spirit and his refusal to do miracles in the Quran (Sura 3:181-84, 4:153, 6:8-9).

Muhammad himself performed no known physical miracles to validate God's message according to the Quran (Surah 17:91-96; 29:47-51). But what about the objective sign of foretelling a future event (i.e. a prophecy)?

A prophecy is a unique and miraculous event in its own right, and if it is specific enough, it could lend powerful support toward Islam's divine claims. A prophetic occurrence would have definitely given due credibility to Muhammad's witness.

The problem is that the sign of prophecy is never used as a sign to verify the prophethood for Muhammad in the Quran. The clearest depiction and strongest evidence for a fulfilled prophecy in the Quran is found in Sura 30:2-4, where a prophecy predicted that the Persians would be defeated by the Roman army at the battle of Issus in "a few years" from the time of the writing. It is true that the Romans did in fact defeat the Persians, but it was not until about fourteen years later. So the prophesied "few years" was a bit of a stretch. There was also already a high chance of this prophecy being true at some point, due to known power of the effective Roman military. This prophecy's vagueness and already high probability doesn't provide us with any substance for Islam's divine claims.

Conclusions Regarding Islam

The Quran stated at one point that signs confirmed authority and yet, on this important point, there seems to be no known supernatural evidences to back up the claims of the Quran itself. The Quran fails in both its own claim for divine authorship, as well as in ours.

The main miraculous claim that is often traditionally used to justify the Quran's divine authorship is the *literary beauty* of the book, which is considered by many Muslims to testify to its divine authorship.

While the skillful writing of an author can truly inspire, this is a fundamentally flawed claim to the miraculous. To make the claim that the Quran is beautifully written is highly subjective and varies from person to person. What would you say to those who happen to find this book distasteful and poorly written? This seems to be an illogical stretch for a Muslim to claim divine authorship of the Quran by using an argument based out of subjective opinion and then calling it miraculous. If the Quran were to have been inspired by God, we *would* expect that it very well might be a beautifully written book, but this is not sufficient evidence by itself. If this were considered divine proof, then any person could make the claim to a wonderfully written literary work—Shakespeare, Dante, Melville, or C.S. Lewis—as divinely inspired.

With the Quran unable to provide any supernatural or objective evidence for its divine authorship, skepticism is natural. We are then safely able to dismiss the Quran as being no different than any other book penned by a man who claims to hear from God. This being the case, we can cease from looking any further into the religion of Islam. Let us move on to consider the religion and writings of the Judeo-Christian God.

The Bible (The Old and New Testaments)

Criterion 1: The message itself would announce the claim of divine inspiration.

The Bible, both Old and New Testaments, was written in the Hebrew, Aramaic, and Greek languages. It loudly claims to be the inspired, inerrant, and infallible Word of God in these *original* languages.

The Bible is not one book, but a collection of sixty-six separate books with various themes, written over a span of more than two thousand years, by over forty different authors from diverse socio-political backgrounds, personalities, vocations, and experiences. These books claim to be the preserved records of God's creation, redemption, and continuous relationship with mankind; God's promises, blessings, judgments, prophecies, fulfillments and other divinely significant historical activities are found documented in both the surface level and the abyssal depths of its pages.

Indeed, the Bible is not shy about its claim to divine authority and authenticity. The Bible admits that God's prophets and their delegates have carefully recorded the Word of God, passage by passage, word by word, letter by letter, all of which is wholly inspired by God, while retaining both the personality and writing styles of each of the book's authors. Here are some self-authenticating claims that attest to the divine inspiration of the scriptures. These scriptures showcase the Bible's qualification for our first criterion—the claim of divine authorship:

The Bible claims to be divinely inspired:
- 1 Thessalonians 2:13: "And we also thank God constantly for this, that when you received the word of God, which

you heard from us, you accepted it not as the word of men but as *what it really is, the word of God, which is at work in you believers.*"

The Bible claims to be sufficient for us to know God:

- 2 Timothy 3:16: "*All Scripture is breathed out by God and profitable for teaching, for reproof, for correction, and for training in righteousness.*"

The Bible claims to be preserved by God:

- Isaiah 40:8: "The grass withers, the flower fades, but *the word of our God will stand forever.*"
- Matthew 24:35: " Heaven and earth will pass away, but *my words will not pass away.*"
- John 10:35: "...*Scripture cannot be broken.*"

The Bible claims to be truthful and inerrant in all of its statements:

- John 17:17: "Sanctify them in the truth; *your word is truth.*"
- Titus 1:1-2: "Paul, a servant of God and an apostle of Jesus Christ, for the sake of the faith of God's elect and their knowledge of the truth, which accords with godliness, in hope of eternal life, *which God, who never lies, promised before the ages began.*"

Criterion 2: The message would contain a miraculous mark of divine communication.

The Bible has passed the first of the criteria—it claims divine authority. Next, we will consider the indicators or supernatural "marks" that we can draw on to validate its divine origin. The verifications for the Bible's divine inspiration are two-fold. First is the significant witness of supernatural knowledge, and the second—and most objective—is fulfilled prophecy. Let's begin with the first witness.

Supernatural knowledge. The Bible is trustworthy in the accuracy of its descriptions of places, people, natural phenomena, and cultural characteristics.

What we find today is that the historical record and forensic sciences involved in Near East archaeological research are favorable toward the Bible's historical claims. The Bible speaks in many places in passing about where certain cities were located, the idols that were worshipped there, the strongholds it possessed, political heads, and even the industries that were commonplace in that stage of history. The Bible records them as simple, well-known facts—facts that came under attack from modern skepticism and yet today many of these truthful scriptural records are now verified at archaeological dig sites.

Once, skeptics thought that the Hittite people and King David of Israel were old Bible myths—yet we now know, through excavations, that the Hittites did in fact exist and that there was a King David of Israel. *Time* magazine has stated that, "Following the 1993 discovery in Israel of a stone containing the inscriptions 'House of David' and 'King of Israel'...skeptics' claim that David never existed is now hard to defend."[13] This is a continuous theme and pattern in the field of archaeology—the Bible says the skeptics doubt, and archaeologists verify the Bible's claim. This is just a single example of the numerous accounts where Near East archaeology have constantly verified the biblical account and reveal the Bible as a trustworthy historical document.

If the physical accuracies can be accounted for as trustworthy, then why question the miraculous events as untrustworthy? Shouldn't we give the Bible the benefit of the doubt? Is our culture's commitment to atheistic naturalism clouding the possible truth of such events, perhaps? Jesus Christ Himself attested to a literal Jonah-and-the-great-fish account

(Matthew 12:39-40), a literal Satan and demons (Matthew 12:26-27), a literal Adam and Eve (Matthew 19:3-6), and a literal Noah with a global flood existing in the past (Matthew 24:37-39), just as the Old Testament declares. If the Bible is God's word, and the physical facts are accurate, then it is reasonable to assume the possibility that even the miraculous events happened just as they are recorded as well.

The Case for a Flood

One such event that skeptics often attack is the event of the global flood. The Bible speaks of the fountains of the deep bursting forth through the Earth's crust (Genesis 7:11), giving way to a worldwide flood that destroyed the ancient world about some 4,400 years ago.

The evidence that we find today to confirm this account of a global flood is everywhere—literally. It is no secret that there are compressed pockets of dead, organic material (coal, oil, mass fossilized graveyards, and isolated dinosaur fossils) cemented in sedimentary rock layers all over the Earth.

Interestingly, even carbon dating evidence has come to the surface lately, challenging old-age evolutionary assumptions. Traces of Carbon-14 have now been found in coal, oil, and *dinosaur bones*. Carbon-14 is a very unstable isotope, which is traceable in anything that has been once living—but only up to about 100,000 years. Simply put, if Carbon-14 is found in any dead organic material, that material can be assumed to have died less than 100,000 years ago, though it is likely much younger than that.

Since traces of this isotope have been found in these creatures, it provides hard scientific evidence that these "prehistoric" creatures are only thousands of years old, and the catastrophe responsible for their burial just as recent. In the biblical account of the worldwide flood, the mighty rushing waters that swept across the Earth provides for us a perfect answer as to why we see once living things buried under wave-like patterns of sedimentary rock on a global scale. One only has to look to the Earth-moving damages caused by recent flood disasters to be convinced of the power of water. The displacement of Spirit Lake at the time of Mount St. Helens' eruption provides such an example.

We also see other geological anomalies on Earth, testifying to that colossal event. Huge trenches have been found, revealing a massive split in the crust of the Earth. Many of these trenches—such as the Mariana Trench—have vents at the bottom of the ocean floor that are continuously pouring forth hot water from within the Earth today. This is exactly where the Bible explains that most of the water of the flood came from. "In the six hundredth year of Noah's life, in the second month, on the seventeenth day of the month, on the same day were all the fountains of the deep broken up, and the windows of heaven were opened" (Genesis 7:11). What is interesting is that the Bible recorded the "fountains of the deep" long before we could scientifically verify it through deep-sea exploration technology. And yet, here it was all along, faithfully recorded in the pages of an ancient scripture that claims divine inspiration.

The Bible also says that the mountains rose during the time of the flood and the valleys sank down (Psalms 104:5-8). Clearly, there was massive tectonic activity going on beneath the floodwaters due to the pressure of the water bursting forth from the Earth. The actions of these mountains rising up and valleys sinking explains why we see fossilized marine life on the tops of mountainous regions all over the world today, including the famous Mount Everest and the mountains of Peru. To find marine life in any mountainous region tells us that the mountains existed at some point under the water, where the marine life once lived and flourished.

If all the mountains were made low and valley basins were at one time non-existent as we know them today, then all of the Earth could have been relatively flatter, and when the flood erupted, the entire Earth could very well have been covered with that amount of water. The water that we currently possess today would be about 2.7 kilometers deep worldwide if the Earth's land mass was flat, making this flood a very real possibility.[14] Where, then, did the water go after the flood? It's still here. The land shifted vertically, giving rise to the continents and mountains that we see today, and the water that was once covering all of the land eventually sank into the valleys that lowered in elevation.

It is also significant that in some mountainous regions, such as the Rocky Mountains, there are curved groove formations observed in the rock called "bent strata." This bending appearance implies that, at one time, the mountains were relatively wavy and soft. Once the bends were formed, the strata hardened very quickly, turning those once-soft bends into hardened rock. The hardening of these types of strata was likely done when the water and hardening minerals mixed and produced a cementing effect. These type of observations are expected if the world underwent a worldwide flood and shifting of the tectonic plates, as recorded in the Bible.

In addition to these observations, Paleontologist Dr. Mary Schweitzer recently discovered a dinosaur fossil that rocked the scientific world and challenged its naturalistic assumptions about the past. Dr. Schweitzer accidentally broke open a Tyrannosaur femur bone and discovered soft tissue, such as *red blood cells and proteins, were still present in the bones!* The implication of this discovery is that this Tyrannosaurus was hunting *thousands* of years ago, not millions. Soft tissue cannot stay preserved for even a million years, let alone the 65 million years that evolution requires. This soft tissue discovery is in perfect consistency with the Bible's account of a recent flood but doesn't line up in the least with naturalism's millions of years.

These evidences and hundreds of others verify the Bible's reliability, putting skeptics in the awkward position of having to invent imaginative theories in an attempt to explain away these facts. Their theories are constantly changing, while the scriptures stand firmly in their facts. It is true that, currently, there are historical questions that will arise and must still be resolved, but as time moves on and archaeology progresses, historical gaps are being closed more and more.

A Supernatural Knowledge of the World

The scriptures provide numerous accounts, mentioned in passing, of advanced knowledge that the relatively primitive biblical authors could not have known experientially. Especially considering what we know about their culture and its lack of technological knowledge, it seems highly unlikely that this knowledge couldn't have come from any human intuition.

It wasn't until the 6th century B.C. that the advanced Greek philosophers begun moving away from the idea that the Earth was a flat disc sitting on water. They began at this time to speculate that the Earth may in fact be circular. Centuries before the Greeks, however, certain books of the Bible that claimed to be inspired by God already had made factual statements concerning the nature of the Earth. The book of Isaiah was one such book that spoke about the Earth being round in a universe in the process of expansion. Consider this passage from Isaiah 40:22-23:

It is He who sits above the circle of the earth,
and its inhabitants are like grasshoppers,
Who stretches out the heavens like a curtain
And spreads them out like a tent to dwell in.

Even the expansion of the universe for thousands of years was recorded. Interestingly, it wasn't until the 1920s, through the invention of the Hubble Telescope, that the scientific discovery of stars expanding was confirmed by observable science.

Another observation noted in Job 26:7, the oldest book of the Bible, states that God,

He stretches out the north over empty space
And hangs the earth on nothing.

This is an early reference to the Earth "hanging on nothing," or what we might describe today as free-floating in space, as spoken from a man who could never have seen the Earth from such heights to verify this claim—unless it was communicated to him from the One who possessed that knowledge.

Another interesting insight was mentioned in the Bible before the knowledge of germs and viruses as the microscopic culprits behind the infectious diseases and sicknesses was widespread. The Bible recorded that *fresh* water or running water must be used in order to cleanse oneself effectively. Leviticus 15:11-13 says of the person who has had an incident of bodily discharge:

Anyone whom the one with the discharge touches without having rinsed his hands in water shall wash his clothes and bathe himself in water and be unclean until the evening. And an earthenware vessel that the one with the discharge touches shall be broken, and every vessel of wood shall be rinsed in water.

And when the one with a discharge is cleansed of his discharge, then he shall count for himself seven days for his cleansing, and wash his clothes. And he shall bathe his body in fresh water and shall be clean.

Washing your hands thoroughly has only becomes a recent medical practice, in order to prevent the spread of diseases to other patients in hospitals, and yet it was commanded thousands of years ago by God to prevent His people from being "unclean."

God additionally speaks in a rhetorical way to Job, proclaiming to him that springs exist in the depths of the ocean. Job 38:16 says, "Have you entered into the springs of the sea, or walked in the recesses of the deep?"

How could the existence of underwater springs have been known thousands of years ago? It has only been within this last century, with the aid of technological advancements, that we are now able to plummet the depths of the ocean floor using sonar. Being aided by high-tech underwater machines, we can now observe the existence of these deep ocean vents that the Bible declared to be fact long ago.

The school's history classes and science departments that rely upon naturalistic assumptions must constantly update their textbooks to suit the constantly changing theories, remove debunked hoaxes, unknowingly add new ones, and change the fluctuating evolutionary dates every few years.

All the while, the Bible remains to be the unchanging constant in the realms of knowledge and wisdom in all that it speaks to. It is a trustworthy book that has been proven to withstand the test of time and skepticism in all its various forms. This is what we would expect to see if this book was indeed inspired by God.

How Did They Receive This Knowledge?

These accounts of advanced knowledge are only a few of a great many that could be listed in support for the supernatural knowledge that the scriptures provide for us. My question for the skeptic at this point is: how could anyone living at that time have known that these things were true? Could it be that when the Israelites claimed to hear from God through prophetic spokesmen like Isaiah and Job that they spoke the truth? If the Bible claims to literally be the words of God, wouldn't fantastic accuracies of knowledge like these be expected? Regardless of where you stand on this issue, these facts most definitely reveal that the Bible is a unique book, far ahead of its time—thousands of years ahead.

I will honestly admit supernatural knowledge doesn't *necessarily* prove God inspired the Bible, but these "outsider" facts are a strange oddity unparalleled in number over any other document of antiquity. Nevertheless, this mysterious knowledge is still a condition that we would be expected to find if the Bible were *truly* inspired by God—we would expect it to be truthful, accurate, and reliable. Let us continue on to the second and most objective evidence that points to the divine inspiration of scripture—prophecy.

What is Prophecy?

Imagine some stranger came up to you and said, "I have a pre-diction from God. In two years, an asteroid is going to hit the Atlantic Ocean and a civil war will break out in Britain." Then imagine that, as you were watching television about the same time two years later, you heard the breaking news report and witnessed documented footage of a small but deadly asteroid that impacted in the Atlantic Ocean alongside another news report of an intense civil war in Britain.

The predictions of the stranger actually came true! But how could it be that he knew about these events so far in advance, especially dates and events that he could have never person-ally set into motion? Are these accurate prophecies from a per-son who knows God, just as he claimed, or is this just a huge coincidence? Either way, this person has become a whole lot more interesting to you. At this point, you might not necessar-ily believe that this person was from God, but you no doubt would begin to think that something is unique and special about this person.

Now, consider that the same stranger came up to you again and said, "I have a message from God for you. God wants you to know that He is watching you and will keep you safe and provide for you. Remember this, because in a few months, you shall receive some very hard news." Now that the person has some credibility from former prophetic predictions, you begin to wonder what might happen or at least if something will happen.

A few months pass, and on a trip to the doctor, he diagno-ses you with cancer; you become bedridden within a month, unable to move due to the pain of the cancer. In the midst of your financial anxieties of paying for your treatments, someone anonymously takes over all of your house bills, car payments, hospital fees, and all other debts. At this point, no doubt the thought would come to you that maybe what the stranger said is true after all. Maybe he does know God as he said.

A year later, you fully recover and you realize that, during that time of hardship, you actually were kept safe and provided for the whole time, just as the stranger told you. That stranger made truthful predictions that were validated by what came to pass—you now have a rational and experiential basis for your belief and trusting in God through the testimony of a prophetic stranger. This prophetic phenomenon is an interwoven characteristic of the Bible, but instead of only seeing few prophecies being fulfilled (as I illustrated in my story), scripture reveals hundreds to marvel at.

Along with the historical witness of the resurrection of Jesus Christ (which will be covered later), the sign of prophecy is the most objective verification for the supernatural nature of the Bible. *Prophetic fulfillment is where a prediction is made of a future event, where the details of that event eventually come to pass.*

The fulfillment of the prophetic predictions in the Bible is an extremely difficult problem to solve with a naturalistic perspective—especially given the very specific nature of the prophecies. Depending on how vague a prediction is, one could simply make the case that, statistically, it was likely to have happened, just as we have previously seen in the battle of Issus in the Quran. Not all prophecies are vague, however. There are many prophetic predictions in the Bible that are *specific in their detail*, and these specifics point us to the God who provided this detailed supernatural knowledge.

God and Prophecy

The biblical nature of divine prophesy is stated in 2 Peter 1:21: "For no prophecy was ever produced by the will of man, but men spoke from God as they were carried along by the Holy Spirit." In other words, a prophetic word as carried out by the man of God was not determined by the will of the prophet himself, but rather, he performed his duty as an agent in carrying out God's message. In this light, and in our discussion so far, prophecy provides for us a sort of litmus test to see whether God may have actually divinely inspired a message to us, since God alone is able to dictate future events.

In ancient Israel, prophets were of utmost importance, since they were God's active voice to the nation. The Old Testament amplified the significance of the role of the prophet by stating that if a prophet was able to perform signs and wonders and their prophecies came to pass with 100% accuracy, then they were indeed to be trusted as God's messengers (Deuteronomy 18:21-22).

If a prophet were ever to make inaccurate predictions, however, they were thereby exposed as a false prophet. A self-proclaimed prophet, falsely deceiving others in the name of God, was sentenced to death, according to God's law in Israel. The role and claim of the prophet, therefore, was no light responsibility to God or the nation, since the prophet carried the holy privilege and awesome responsibility of declaring God's direction to His people. Therefore, it is natural that a serious penalty would be given to any deceiver who claims to be of God and makes false claims on His behalf. In this way, through predictive prophecy, signs, and wonders, God made sure that His people had a way to know if a message was authentically from Him and keep them from the deceptions of men.

Now, if we used God's own standard in the Bible for the one hundred percent truthfulness of a fulfillment (which is a reasonable standard by anyone's estimation), then we likewise ought to see an immaculate track record of prophecy throughout God's book—the Bible. What follows below are specific prophecies that provide authentication to divine authorship.

1) The prophecy of the destruction of the ancient city of Tyre, located in Ezekiel 26:3-14. This prophecy was written through the prophet Ezekiel in approximately 580 B.C. It says, concerning the great city:

Therefore thus says the Lord God: Behold, I am against you, O Tyre, and will bring up many nations against you, as the sea brings up its waves. They shall destroy the walls of Tyre and break down her towers, and I will scrape her soil from her and make her a bare rock. She shall be in the midst of the sea a place for the spreading of nets, for I have spoken, declares the Lord God. And she shall become plunder for the nations, and her daughters on the mainland shall be killed by the sword. Then they will know that I am the Lord.

For thus says the Lord God: Behold, I will bring against Tyre from the north Nebuchadnezzar king of Babylon, king of kings, with horses and chariots, and with horsemen and a host of many soldiers. He will kill with the sword your daughters on the mainland. He will set up a siege wall against you and throw up a mound against you, and raise a roof of shields against you. He will direct the shock of his battering rams against your walls, and with his axes he will break down your towers. His horses will be so many that their dust will cover you. Your walls will shake at the noise of the horsemen and wagons and chariots, when he enters your gates as men enter a city that has been breached. With the hoofs of his horses he will trample all your streets. He will kill your people with the sword, and your mighty pillars will fall to the ground. They will plunder your riches and loot your merchandise. They will break down your walls and destroy your pleasant houses. Your stones and timber and soil they will cast into the midst of the waters. And I will stop the music of your songs, and the sound of your lyres shall be heard no more. I will make you a bare rock. You shall be a place for the spreading of nets. You shall never be rebuilt, for I am the Lord; I have spoken, declares the Lord God.

This prophecy is one of the most specific prophecies in the Bible. The conquering Babylonian empire partially fulfilled this prophecy by destroying the mainland settlement of Tyre after a long siege in 585-573 B.C. After the pillage of the Babylonians, all that was left of the city was a populated section of the city on a small island just off the coast.

Alexander the Great also attacked Tyre in 332 B.C., and it was here that Alexander gave the inhabitants no mercy. By taking stones, timber, and dirt from the city's ruins on the mainland, Alexander made a land bridge to get to the island. Using this land bridge, Alexander's troops stormed into the city, destroying it completely. All residents were either killed or sold into slavery.

Today, there is only a partial ruin from this original city left, and it became a small place for fishermen—for the "spread of nets," just as was prophesied thousands of years before by God's prophet Ezekiel.

2) The future prediction of conquering empires of Daniel 2:31-42 and 7:1-7, 15-18 contains a strikingly accurate prediction in approximately 605-539 B.C. In the Bible, God gives the prophet Daniel the ability to describe and interpret to King Nebuchadnezzar his prophetic dream of a mysterious layered statue. Daniel interprets the dream of the Babylonian king by saying:

You saw, O king, and behold, a great image. This image, mighty and of exceeding brightness, stood before you, and its

*appearance was frightening. The head of this image was of
fine gold, its chest and arms of silver, its middle and thighs of
bronze, its legs of iron, its feet partly of iron and partly of clay.
As you looked, a stone was cut out by no human hand, and it
struck the image on its feet of iron and clay, and broke them
in pieces. Then the iron, the clay, the bronze, the silver, and
the gold, all together were broken in pieces, and became like
the chaff of the summer threshing floors; and the wind carried
them away, so that not a trace of them could be found. But the
stone that struck the image became a great mountain and filled
the whole earth. This was the dream. Now we will tell the king
its interpretation. You, O king, the king of kings, to whom the
God of heaven has given the kingdom, the power, and the might,
and the glory, and into whose hand he has given, wherever they
dwell, the children of man, the beasts of the field, and the birds
of the heavens, making you rule over them all—you are the
head of gold. Another kingdom inferior to you shall arise after
you, and yet a third kingdom of bronze, which shall rule over all
the earth. And there shall be a fourth kingdom, strong as iron,
because iron breaks to pieces and shatters all things. And like
iron that crushes, it shall break and crush all these. And as you
saw the feet and toes, partly of potter's clay and partly of iron,
it shall be a divided kingdom, but some of the firmness of iron
shall be in it, just as you saw iron mixed with the soft clay. And
as the toes of the feet were partly iron and partly clay, so the
kingdom shall be partly strong and partly brittle."*

The prophetic dream predicted that an inferior kingdom associated with the lion and silver would usurp
the empire of Babylon. Afterwards, a third and stronger
kingdom would reign over that inferior kingdom, associ-
ating with the bear and bronze. Then, after that kingdom,
a fourth and final kingdom would appear to crush the
third. The characteristics of these succeeding empires
have long been associated to those empires that historically have followed the major empires that came after

Babylon along with their associated animal "mascots."
The Medo-Persian Empire is the lion with silver, the Greek
Empire with her bear and bronze, and finally, the fourth
cruel and crushing Roman Empire.

These predictions have been so accurate and precise
that even many critics are in agreement that Daniel was
indeed accurately referencing the future conquests of
these kingdoms, in exact order, with stunning accuracy.
The historical data is on Daniel's side.

Many have since tried to attribute Daniel's accuracy
by claiming that the text was written after the conquests
had already occurred. This attempt to explain away this
supernatural accuracy has been in vain, since this accu-
sation is unsubstantiated; even the most liberal dating of
the book of Daniel firmly points to it being written before
this prophecy's fulfillment.

3) *Persian King Cyrus was mentioned by name before he
was even born in Isaiah 44:28-45:1.* In approximately
740-690 B.C., the book of Isaiah recorded these words:

Who says of Cyrus, "He is my shepherd,
and he shall fulfill all my purpose";
saying of Jerusalem, "She shall be built,"
and of the temple, "Your foundation shall be laid."

Thus says the Lord to his anointed, to Cyrus,
whose right hand I have grasped,
to subdue nations before him
and to loose the belts of kings,
to open doors before him
that gates may not be closed."

God told Isaiah that an anointed man named Cyrus
would be the Lord's servant and an instrument in the
rebuilding of Jerusalem and the Lord's Temple, whose

destruction was accomplished through the Babylonian Empire.

These events (the building of the Temple and the construction of Jerusalem) took place exactly as was prophesied—under the Persian King Cyrus 150 years after the prediction was made. There is simply no human way for Isaiah to have known this information about these future events (including the personal name of the king that was still yet to be born), unless Isaiah was in fact in communication with God, just as he said he was. God alone knew how the orchestration of the future events would transpire. Isaiah was in communication with this God.

4) *The prophecy of Israel's return to their land* is one of the most interesting prophecies that can actually be attested today. All throughout the Bible, predictions have been made, stating that one day, the Jewish people would be scattered throughout the world due to their disobedience against God (Deuteronomy 28:64-68). In Luke 21:20-24, we see this prediction of their periodic exile:

> *But when you see Jerusalem surrounded by armies, then know that its desolation has come near. Then let those who are in Judea flee to the mountains, and let those who are inside the city depart, and let not those who are out in the country enter it, for these are days of vengeance, to fulfill all that is written. Alas for women who are pregnant and for those who are nursing infants in those days! For there will be great distress upon the earth and wrath against this people. They will fall by the edge of the sword and be led captive among all nations, and Jerusalem will be trampled underfoot by the Gentiles, until the times of the Gentiles are fulfilled.*

When the Roman army sacked the Jewish temple in 70 A.D., only decades after Jesus' death, The Jews declared war and revolted. The Romans responded to

JEFF McCONNELL

the Jewish threat by destroying Jerusalem and mas-
sacring the Jewish people in the first of many future
holocausts that the Jews historically faced. Many of the
remaining and escaping Jewish people fled from their
homeland and spread into numerous Jewish communities around the Mediterranean world. This occurrence
is historically referred to as the *diaspora*, which literally
means the "scattering."

Yet, through all of the anti-Semitic peril that they faced
as a former people of God, this Hebrew people miraculously and successfully preserved aspects of their distinct
culture, beliefs, and language through the centuries of
homelessness and trials.

Finally, after many centuries of exile and fighting for
their own existence, Israel returned to their homeland and
became a nation again in 1948, after suffering through
the horror of their latest holocaust at the hands of the
Nazis in World War II. The returning of Israel to their
homeland was prophesied in many places in the Bible,
but largely in Ezekiel 36:22-24 and Isaiah 11:11-12,
which tells of God's plan to reclaim this people:

*In that day the Lord will extend his hand yet a second time to
recover the remnant that remains of his people, from Assyria,
from Egypt, from Pathros, from Cush, from Elam, from Shinar,
from Hamath, and from the coastlands of the sea.*

*He will raise a signal for the nations
and will assemble the banished of Israel,
and gather the dispersed of Judah
from the four corners of the earth.*

Large numbers of Jews have indeed flocked back to their Palestinian home from all the ends of the Earth, as was prophesied would happen. In this way, the Hebrew people themselves are a most convincing evidence, not only to the reality of their God (Yahweh) being the true God, but of the faithful, promise-keeping nature of God.

Conquered or fleeing peoples tend to integrate into their surrounding culture and begin adopting the customs and beliefs of the dominant culture—thus eventually losing their national and cultural identity. Generation after generation, a conquered people become more and more integrated and their identity lessens and lessens, until after about four or five generations, their cultural distinctions begin to disappear altogether. This has been the case of many people groups. But despite all of the odds, after almost two thousand years of wandering in other countries, God preserved them as He promised He would do and has plans for them alongside God's Gentile or non-Jewish believing remnant, just as stated in Deuteronomy 4:27-31:

And the Lord will scatter you among the peoples, and you will be left few in number among the nations where the Lord will drive you. And there you will serve gods of wood and stone, the work of human hands, that neither see, nor hear, nor eat, nor smell. But from there you will seek the Lord your God and you will find him, if you search after him with all your heart and with all your soul. When you are in tribulation, and all these things come upon you in the latter days, you will return to the Lord your God and obey his voice. For the Lord your God is a merciful God. He will not leave you or destroy you or forget the covenant with your fathers that he swore to them.

The Reliability of the Bible

The reliability of the Bible is an enormous topic—far beyond the scope of this writing—but before I speak to it, I want to make this statement regarding the accusations of contradictions: the inspiration of scripture does not contain a single alleged contradiction that hasn't been already adequately resolved by scholarship over the centuries. There is no shortage of books dedicated to debunking the skeptical claims of contradictions in the Bible. If one is interested, I personally recommend *The Big Book of Bible Difficulties* by Dr. Norma L. Geisler, which contains reasonable answers to a large portion of seemingly irreconcilable passages.

It has also been my experience, as a former skeptic myself, that many of the Bible's difficulties that I once used to discount the Bible are actually easily eliminated when taking into consideration the style of writing, surrounding cultural contexts, and numerous forms of figures of speech common to Hebrew and Greek culture at the time of its writing.

Old Testament Reliability

One question is worthy of discussion at this point. Even if the Bible was God's word, how do we know the English translations we read today remained faithful to the original, inspired manuscripts through the centuries? Haven't changes been made that would challenge the divine authority of the Bible that we read today? It is here that we will look to both the Old and New Testaments to better understand how the scriptures were preserved. In the case of Old Testament transmission accuracy, we can look to the evidence of what has been called the *Dead Sea*

Scrolls, found between 1946 and 1956 at Wadi Qumran, near the area of the Dead Sea. The Dead Sea Scrolls were translated by a devout separatist sect of Jews called the Essenes before the time of Christ. These passionate Jews sought to preserve the Old Testament and other important writings from the rising threat of the Roman Empire and increasingly liberal Jews who were compromising their culture by adapting to Roman ideas.

The Dead Sea Scrolls contained the complete Old Testament (except for the book of Esther) and have been compared to numerous other Old Testament manuscripts we have available today. The Dead Sea Scroll texts and our current texts reveal that our numerous copies that were made throughout the ages are still essentially identical in transmission. This provides for us a great insight into the incredible preservation of these ancient manuscripts and the reliability of that ancient tradesman (the scribe) whose sole discipline was to meticulously copy documents with precision.

This find has disproven and refuted the common objection regarding the Old Testament portion of the Bible being full of errors and changes. What we have today is the same quality of manuscripts that Jesus Christ claimed were divinely inspired, inerrant and trustworthy two thousand years ago.

New Testament Reliability

As for the authentication of the New Testament, we have an even greater advantage of knowing its accuracy, because we are in the current possession of over 5,000 copies of New Testament manuscripts for reference. Some of these copies are as early as the first century (during the time of the apostles) and the second century (during the time of those who followed in the teaching of the original apostles).

This staggering amount of preserved manuscripts is unparalleled in any ancient writings. The next greatest amount of copied manuscripts is 642 copies of Homer's *Iliad*. We have even fewer copies of Plato's works or the records of Julius Caesar. This marks the New Testament as by far the best-preserved text in the ancient world.

We can be extremely confident that the New Testament is accurate as to the essence of the original documents simply by referencing the numerous copies, which make it easier for textual scholars to use the process of elimination in removing scribal errors, spelling mistakes, or any other additions found in the translated texts.

For an example of this process of eliminating the scribal errors, let's use the example phrase "the cat is black." Let's say that we are translators that uncover, from an archaeological dig site, five old papyrus paper parchments that contain this phrase transmitted from an unknown original document. The phrases on the five papyrus papers read:

Papyrus #1: "the cat is black"
Papyrus #2: "the kat is black"
Papyrus #3: "the cat is black"
Papyrus #4: "the cat is green"
Papyrus #5: "the cat is black"

With these five scriptures laid out side by side, a scholar can come to a reasonable conclusion on what the original scripture must have said that those scribes used to write Papyrus 1-5. They do this through the elimination of obvious mistakes by referencing the other copies.

For example, in Papyrus #2, we have found a misspelled word. The word "cat", spelt with a "k". We know this misspelling is an error simply because the other four texts do not contain that same variation. The majority of the other manuscripts read the same when it comes to the word "cat" but Papyrus #2 reads differently. Because we have access to the other manuscripts, we have a far better ability to determine what the original spelling must have been and rule out any error. Thus, it is most likely that the spelling of the word "kat" in Papyrus #2 is the wrong spelling—a scribal error.

The same can be said with the error in Papyrus #4. It is clear from the majority that the cat was indeed black, so if one text out of the five says it was green, we can reasonably conclude that Papyrus #4 contains the error. The more manuscripts we possess, the more easily the original word or sentences can be separated from scribal errors. By taking into consideration all of the manuscripts that are available, these errors can be removed and a final perfected translation can be produced, true to the original document. This is how scholars distinguish error from truth with ancient documents, including the Bible, and they are able to do so quite efficiently—especially with thousands of copies to observe, not just five!

While errors do exist in the ancient manuscripts, those errors are relatively minor and similar to what we have just seen in the "cat" papyrus illustration. Spelling or word position in a sentence are the most common variations, and it is noteworthy that no single error found in the texts of the Bible has been significant enough to have jeopardized any long-held doctrines in the Christian church. Areas such as the attributes of God, the deity of Christ, salvation, sin, Christ's resurrection and second coming, eternity, paradise, Hell, etc. are all teachings left unscathed by the minor transmission errors.

It remains a provable fact that nothing dramatic has been changed with the text of scripture, with the exception of a couple major additions worth noting. As for these possible additions, both are located in the Gospels. One is in the fast-paced concluding verses of Mark 16, in verses 9-20; the other is found in John 7:53-8:11, where an account was recorded of Jesus' interaction with the woman caught in adultery about to be stoned. These sections of scripture are not found in our earliest texts. Whether these are legitimate additions or not, they remove nothing of any major doctrinal significance from the Bible.

These possible additions of scripture are also transparently footnoted in most Bibles (especially study Bibles) so that the reader is not ignorant of these or any other significant translation issues. With this information presented on the pages of the English translations, one is able to either accept or reject the addition as originally being part of God's word. At the very least, whether you accept those possible additions or not, when you hold the modern Greek and Hebrew Bible, you are in possession of the equivalent of the original manuscripts of the Bible. To continue believing that the Bible is unreliable despite the thousands of copied manuscripts as evidence, logically, one must also discard all ancient historical documents as being equally unreliable myth.

If God has written in scripture, then surely He is able to assure us the accuracy and preservation of His word. And as you can see, thousands of copies were widespread throughout the Roman Empire in such a way that no monopoly on the scriptures could ever be accomplished. No single scribe's error could be imposed upon the text either, without the sheer number of manuscripts exposing it!

The ancient history of the Bible's transmission and preservation is a perfect protection plan for all of those who hope to be able to benefit from an accurate word of God. Through the carelessness of human nature and destructive enemies of God's message, the Bible continuously remains to be a miracle of divine preservation under the protection of its Divine Author. If this book is of God, we would expect nothing less than its supernatural preservation. Interestingly enough, the Bible reveals in Isaiah 40:8 that the words of God would not fade but stand forever: "The grass withers, the flower fades, but the word of our God will stand forever."

Has God Revealed Himself?

In examining the claims of the Quran and the Bible, the Bible remains superior in our expected criteria for the supernatural revelation of God. One could explore the prophecies of scripture more extensively only to find that the weight of its supernatural origin increases in strength and probability, making it irrational for anyone to deny the divine influence of scripture. When adding the historical accuracies, supernatural features, and prophetic fulfillments together, we can see that it is a very reasonable position for a person to take when they suppose the Bible to be the Word of God. It is therefore also rational to trust in the physical and spiritual truths that the Bible speaks on. Its description regarding the topics of God, sin, holiness, Heaven, Hell, love, promises, the promised Messiah, the cross, atonement for sin, God's justice and righteousness, our need for forgiveness, and so forth ought be taken very seriously as well. While it is true that a historian's book can get the historical facts right but interpret the message of history wrongly, this cannot be said of a book that possesses the evidence of divine authorship—the Author who created everything is the only one qualified to interpret that reality correctly.

Fulfilled prophecy logically implies the fact that an omniscient (all-knowing), intelligent Being exists who is capable of informing man of unfolding future events—things that finite and time-stricken creatures could never know. If one wishes to discount the Bible at this point, then one must explain the accuracy of these and numerous other prophecies recorded in the Bible. The skeptic's explanation of these transcendent prophecies is a task that is yet to be completed persuasively and must be done in order to begin to disprove the Bible's claim of divine inspiration.

It is therefore reasonable for the seeker of truth to assume that the God of Creation has indeed revealed Himself through not only the natural world, as we have walked through in the first two chapters, but also in the realm of numerous accounts of supernatural knowledge and prophetic predictions as found in the Bible.

Judaism and Christianity

Both Judaism and Christianity hold that the Old Testament is the Word of God. The Old Testament is the historical record of how God and man were alienated from each other through sin. In it, God created a nation (Israel) to become His covenant people through faith and obedience. Through the descendants of Israel, a prophesied Messiah was appointed to come to reconcile us to God and repair our broken relationship.

Judaism does not believe that this prophesied Messiah has arrived yet—they are still waiting for this figure today. Christianity, on the other hand, believes that the long-awaited

Messiah already came and fulfilled the prophecies that were spoken about Him in the Old Testament through the person of Jesus Christ.

Eyewitnesses and dedicated disciples recorded some of Christ's major life events and sayings in the New Testament historical record. If the New Testament's account of Jesus' messianic identity match the Old Testament prophesies about the Messiah, and if the resurrection event is historically factual, then Christianity would rationally prove to be the dominant worldview.

The New Testament already claims divine inspiration (the first of our criteria) in the passages we cited earlier (Matthew 24:35, John 10:35, 17:17, 1 Thessalonians 2:13, Titus 1:1-2, 2 Peter 1:20-21, 2 Timothy 3:16, Revelation 22:18-19). But now, the most impressive criterion for God's special revelation is still yet to come—the reliability of the resurrection testimony and the messianic prophesies of Jesus Christ.

6

A Testimony to the
Resurrection of
JESUS CHRIST

*No testimony is sufficient to establish a miracle, unless the testimony be
of such a kind, that its falsehood would be more miraculous than the fact
which it endeavors to establish.*

DAVID HUME

*And taking the twelve, he said to them, 'See, we are going up to Jerusalem,
and everything that is written about the Son of Man by the prophets will
be accomplished. For he will be delivered over to the Gentiles and will be
mocked and shamefully treated and spit upon. And after flogging him, they
will kill him, and on the third day he will rise.'*

LUKE 18:31-33

History undeniably records manuscript evidence, early
church writings, and the writings of ancient skeptics
that Jesus Christ in fact lived and ministered two thousand years ago in Israel. There is no debate here—this is an
undeniable, historical fact. During this time, the Roman Empire
was ruling the Judaic region with Herod the Great overseeing

the area—the appointed puppet king of Rome. Jesus was baptized at approximately the age of thirty by John the Baptist, and from there, He began His unique three-year ministry that would make Him the most influential, offensive, and widely-known person the world has ever known.

Jesus' life was unique and equipped with great acts of charity, compassion, and numerous miraculous accounts. The gospel of John opens with the bold words about Christ being not only the Son of man, but truly God in the flesh, the second member of the Godhead or *Trinity*, according to Christian theology: "In the beginning was the Word (Jesus Christ), and the Word was with God, and *the Word was God*."

John further supports the divine claim of Christ in 20:27-29, through a conversation between Jesus and His once unbelieving disciple Thomas. In this moment, Jesus Christ appears before the awestruck Thomas and says, "Put your finger here, and see my hands; and put out your hand, and place it in my side. Do not disbelieve, but believe." Thomas answered him, "*My Lord and my God!*" Jesus said to him, "Have you believed because you have seen me? Blessed are those who have not seen and yet have believed." Here, Christ commends Thomas' believing recognition of His Lordship and deity—the disciple trusts in Him.

Christ is recorded to have lived righteously free of sin, which ought to be expected if He were truly God, since God is a Being that is perfectly moral and upright in character. In 1 Peter 2:22, Christ's uncompromising speech was accounted for: "He committed no sin, neither was deceit found in His mouth." There are also other ways in which divinity was assumed or attributed to Him.

- He was worshipped at His birth (Matthew 2:11) and accepted worship during His earthly reign (Matthew 28:9).

- He forgave sin, which could only be done if He was God (Matthew 9:2).
- All the elements of Earth obeyed His voice as though He were God (Matthew 8:27).
- He claimed to be the ultimate Judge of all men, assuming a judgment seat role for God alone (Matthew 25:31-33).
- He received names attributed to God in the Old Testament, such as The First and The Last (Isaiah 45:21/Revelation 1:7) and Savior (Isaiah 43:11/Titus 2:13).

Many clearly saw Christ as divine, but what did He claim of Himself? We have this answer in John 10:30, where Jesus was walking in the temple and a group of Jews gathered around Him. It was here that Jesus made this scandalous claim: "I and the Father are one." This word for "one" meant that Christ was claiming a unity of essence with God the Father.

By this statement, Jesus implied that He possesses the same nature of God, and for this claim, the next verse says that the Jews picked up stones to stone Him. Stoning was the death penalty for blasphemy, according to Jewish law. His words were blasphemous because Jesus, being only a mere man (or so they thought), claimed also to be God, which is an utterly unthinkable claim to make, according to the Jews.

After responding to them, Jesus makes another extremely important statement for our purposes. Jesus says in verse 37, "If I do not do the works of my Father, do not believe Me; but if I do them... believe the works so that you may know and understand that the Father is in Me, and I in the Father." Jesus is essentially saying that "my works (miracles) verify who I say I am. If God weren't with me, then God wouldn't be confirming me in the least through any miracles." But God did showcase the wonders of Christ, and it is based off of these wonders that we can make a rational case that Christ was divine.

Truly, this Jesus whom the Bible claims to be divine and sinless is the most fascinating and interesting figure in the history of the world.

Jesus the Miracle Worker

One won't have to venture far into their reading of the Gospels to notice the repetitiveness of miraculous events being traced directly or indirectly to the person of Christ. Through Christ's power, the blind saw, the deaf heard, the mute spoke, people were raised back to life, and the elements of nature were tamed—all through the awesome power that He possessed.

Christ says in John 5:36:

But the testimony that I have is greater than that of John. For the works that the Father has given me to accomplish, the very works that I am doing, bear witness about me that the Father has sent me."

These miracles were not random but a purposeful demonstration so that everyone might know that He was speaking and serving God the Father.

Had Christ not been surrounded by the miraculous, He likely wouldn't have gathered the followers and fame that He did. Jesus was taken seriously but not due to earthly charisma or personality traits that are common to man—for the Jews had many of this sort that history has long since forgotten. All of Israel wondered about who He was and how He could possess such power; even His enemies never could deny this power but insisted that He possessed a power from the devil.

If a man today claimed to be from God, I would assume him to be a lunatic, but if—out of compassion—he healed a person affected with a visible, physical disability in front of my very eyes, I would then begin to listen intently to whatever it was that this man had to say. Healing another person is a great set of divine credentials to have in order to get people to listen to what you have to say! This is what, in fact, did happen—and the world has never gotten over these events, even two thousand years later.

The same standard of miraculous criteria that we are using to identify the divine inspiration of scripture was historically applied to the person of Jesus Christ. Because of these public miracles, many had no other choice but to conclude that He was a prophet of God, and some even realized that He was not just a prophet, but God veiled in human flesh.

The Last Days of Jesus

In the last days of Jesus' ministry, He was caught by the religious leaders (the Pharisees) and sent to the cross, enduring humiliation and ridicule. He was tried, tortured, abused, scourged, and condemned to die a criminal's death—death by crucifixion—just outside the gates of Jerusalem. At this time, His most devout followers abandoned Him: "But all this has taken place *that the Scriptures of the prophets might be fulfilled.* Then all the disciples left him and fled" (Matthew 26:56).

After they had fled, Jesus likely died of asphyxiation, resulting from prolonged crucifixion, and was buried in a rich man's tomb. From this tomb, He rose from the dead three days later in a new, glorified body. In this new body, He appeared to hundreds of people at a time and to His disciples numerous times in the span of forty days before finally ascending into Heaven, back to God.

The Witnesses of the Resurrection

Is there any historical proof available to back up the claims of Jesus' identity as the Son of God? Well, in a court system, we acknowledge that the evidence that carries weight is the collaborating testimonies of one or more eyewitnesses.

Two eyewitnesses can seal the fate of a murderer and place him firmly upon death row, and obviously, the greater the number of testimonies, the more solid a case becomes—the more solid the case becomes, the more certain the conclusion can be because of story collaboration. We know that as long as the witnesses share a common or similar description of the events, we can then gather that information together to organize and piece together the basic truth and timeline of the events. This is what police officers must do in investigating a crime, and this is also what theologians and historians must do (and have done) with the witnesses in the case for the resurrection.

In scripture, we have not one or two but four written eye-witness records of the life, claims, death, and resurrection of Jesus Christ. These testimonies are found in the four Gospels: Matthew, Mark, Luke, and John.

The four Gospels' collective account of the events concerning the empty tomb and the resurrection can be harmonized in this way: Mary Magdalene and a group of women were the first people recorded to have seen the Messiah's tomb empty (Matthew 28:5-6, Mark 16: 4-6, John 20:1). After the women left the tomb, Peter and John also went down inside the tomb where Jesus was placed. Within the tomb, Peter and John witnessed the burial clothes that Christ wore following the crucifixion folded neatly in place (John 20:3-8). The women then walked back to where the disciples had gathered, and along the way, reportedly saw Jesus alive again in His physical body and worshipped Him (Matt 28:9-10). After this first encounter with the resurrected Jesus, Christ walked and taught two other disciples, as they were with Him on the road to Emmaus (Mark 16:12, Luke 24:13-21). At some point after this occurrence, ten of the disciples saw Jesus appear to them in bodily form (Mark 16:14; Luke 24:35-49), and then again later, with a formerly skeptical disciple (Thomas) in attendance, who would not believe until he touched the body of Christ for himself (John 20:28). There was also an occurrence at some point, where Jesus appeared in front of five hundred people at a time, which was mentioned later by Paul in 1 Corinthians 15:6-8:

> Then he appeared to **more than five hundred** brothers at one time, **most of whom are still alive,** though some have fallen asleep. Then he appeared to James, then to all the apostles. Last of all, as to one untimely born, he appeared also to me.

Paul said that many of those people who Christ appeared before were still alive during the writing of his first letter to the Corinthians. Paul therefore implies that anyone who would question Paul's integrity in his statement of the resurrection would be able to verify the truth of his claim by speaking face-to-face with the witnesses who were still alive at that time. In essence, Paul is saying "If you don't believe me, then ask those who have seen Him; they will also verify the truth of what I am saying."

The Resurrection in the Early Church

This resurrection was so important in the early church, that even our first recorded messages preached by the apostles were lathered with the announcement of the resurrection as our divine confirmation to the truth of who Christ was—our Savior and Lord (Acts 2:23-33, 4:10, 10:39-41, 13:29-31, 17:31-34). The resurrection, according to Paul, also verified the truth of Jesus' claims of being not only the Son of God, but God Himself as the second person in the Holy Trinity (three distinct persons: Father, Son, and Holy Spirit, in one divine essence: God).

If a person could successfully disprove the fact of the resurrection, then they can successfully lay the death blow at the base of the Christian faith. The apostle Paul even confirms this in 1 Corinthians 15:14-19:

> And if Christ has not been raised, then our preaching is in vain and your **faith is in vain.** We are even found to be misrepresenting God, because we testified about God that he raised Christ, whom he did not raise if it is true that the dead are not raised. For if the dead are not raised, not even Christ has been raised. And if Christ has not been raised, your **faith is futile** and you are still in your sins. Then those also who have fallen asleep in Christ have perished. If in Christ we have hope in this life only, **we are of all people most to be pitied.**

Was the Resurrection a Hallucination?

There are many reasons why people reject the resurrection, and there are many naturalistic objections that have been put forward in an attempt to disregard the truth of the Bible. One common objection to the resurrection testimony is the theory that the disciples never truly saw Jesus, but instead experienced a hallucination. The problem is that, given the circumstances surrounding the resurrection, hallucinations are a highly implausible and doubtful explanation for the appearances of Christ. The conditions surrounding the resurrection simply don't provide a fitting environment for hallucinations to take place. Most hallucinations are solitary experiences; groups of people don't share the same experiences of mind, since hallucinations affect each mind in different ways. In addition, none of the disciples anticipated the resurrection, which is a pre-condition for a hallucination to take effect—the expectation that something would happen. The reality is that the resurrection shocked Jesus' followers as much as it would shock any one of us today. It was shocking because it happened.

The Resurrection Evidence

The church literally exists today because of the significance of the resurrection of Jesus. The moment a Christian ceases to believe in this key historical event is the moment they cease to be identified as "Christian." The credibility of the resurrection, therefore, must be seen as an essential linchpin to the reliability and truthfulness of the Christian religion. It is a reliability gauged through first-hand eyewitness support as found in the gospels in the New Testament. Consider these direct and indirect evidences that support the testimony of these eyewitnesses:

1) The witnesses are all consistent with the details surrounding the events of the resurrection. Detailed descriptions of the area and locations where some of the encounters of Christ were experienced are consistent with each other's accounts.

2) The transformation of the disciples is also one of the most compelling evidences of the resurrection. These men had

formerly followed Jesus closely for three years, until the authorities finally arrested him. After the arrest was made, they fled as cowards from their Savior, abandoning Him to a shameful fate on a cross.

After they had encountered the risen Christ, God sent His Holy Spirit to fill them with the boldness required to proclaim the message of the resurrected Christ in the face of the horrific persecution that was to come. History and church tradition record that many of the twelve apostles suffered terribly and were ultimately tortured, killed, or both for their commitment to spreading the message of the kingdom of God and the resurrection of Jesus of Nazareth.

Here is why this evidence is important. People don't die for what *they think* is a lie. They might die mistakenly, assuming something to be true that isn't, but they won't die for what *they think* is a lie. This means that, in order for them to have been willing to lay down their lives for this resurrection message, they must have all been undeniably convinced in each of their own minds that they truly did encounter the risen Christ. So convinced of that encounter were they, that they willingly paid for it with their own blood.

On top of that, the moral profile of these individuals doesn't seem to match with that of deceitful liars. These men were culturally Jewish in their upbringing. This morally-strict religious culture would have been heavily ingrained into their Jewish consciences throughout their entire lives, which includes the commandment not to lie. Their personal interests would have also been morally linked to Christ, who spent large amounts of His time centering His teachings upon the ethical truths of God and moral responsibility.

These considerations must be key factors in establishing the moral profiles of the apostles. These moral contexts and interests seem to indicate that they were not the type of people interested in the widespread deception of others. When all is said and done, these men simply do not fit the character profile of those who would lie or fabricate a resurrection story.

3) *The conviction to follow Christ at the expense of opposing traditions* gives us insight into what kind of commitment these men must have had in order to believe in the resurrection of Christ.

Before the disciples became followers of Christ, they were common Jews deeply devoted to the traditional and religious honoring of the Lord's Sabbath Day, which fell on Saturday. Yet, after the resurrection, a notable change transpired with the worship of the Lord among the Christian sects. Worship changed from the last day of the week (Saturday) to the first day of the week (Sunday), the day when Christ rose from the grave. The Jewish followers of Christ began to gather for worship on Sundays instead of Saturdays. By doing this act, they turned themselves away from the deeply ingrained Jewish Sabbath Day tradition and risked judgment and disapproval from those who they desired to reach.

To worship God on a Sunday instead of the Sabbath would have made it extremely difficult for any disciples still living in these Jewish communities. Given the religious devotion of the Jewish people, these committed disciples would likely not have risked the possibility of persecution and alienation by worshipping on a different day if the resurrection of Christ were not an essential core belief of their faith and worth the cost.

4) Ancient, non-Christian sources gave written accounts
of the widespread knowledge of the resurrection. This
is documented proof that the rumors of the resurrection
were widespread around the Roman Empire shortly after
the events had taken place. Consider just one of these
sources, written in 93-94 A.D. by the ancient Jewish historian Josephus in his Antiquities 18.63-64:

*Now there was about this time Jesus, a wise man if it be lawful
to call him a man, for he was a doer of wonders, a teacher of
such men as receive the truth with pleasure. He drew many
after him both of the Jews and the gentiles. He was the Christ.
When Pilate, at the suggestion of the principal men among us,
had condemned him to the cross, those that loved him at the
first did not forsake him, for he appeared to them alive again
the third day, as the divine prophets had foretold these and
then thousand other wonderful things about him and the tribe
of Christians, so named from him, are not extinct at this day.*

This is a very early, yet secular, non-believing Jewish
source, a contemporary of John the apostle, commenting
on the life, death, and resurrection of Jesus Christ. This
statement was written as common, historical knowledge
from a Jewish non-Christian historian for the archives of
Jewish history. Jesus' resurrection is thus as reliable a historical fact as any other written down by any other early
historians in the annals of history.

The Historical Case for the Resurrection

It is interesting to note that some of history's most qualified
legal professionals have declared the same conclusion concerning their examinations of the resurrection. The resurrection has convinced attorney generals such as John Singleton

Cropley, professors like Dr. Paul Maier (a professor of ancient history), skeptical lawyers such as Dr. Frank Morison, and the famous professor and co-founder of Law at Harvard University, Dr. Simon Geenleaf, a former agnostic, who authored one of the greatest authoritative books on legal procedure, *A Treatise on the Law of Evidence*. Dr. Greenleaf said, in his conclusion, of the resurrection:

> *Let the witnesses be compared with themselves, with each other, and with the surrounding facts and circumstances; and let their testimony be sifted, as if it were given in a court of justice, on the side of the adverse party, the witnesses being subjected to a rigorous cross-examination. The result, it is confidently believed, will be an undoubting conviction of their integrity, ability and truth... Either the men of Galilee were men of superlative wisdom, and extensive knowledge and experience, and of deeper skill in the arts of deception, than any and all others, before or after them, or they have truly stated the astonishing things which they saw and heard.[15]*

Arguably the greatest lawyer of British history, Sir Lionel Luckhoo, likewise spoke about the testimony of the resurrection of Jesus Christ saying,

> *I humbly add I have spent more than 42 years as a defense trial lawyer appearing in many parts of the world and am still in active practice. I have been fortunate to secure a number of successes in jury trials and I say unequivocally the evidence for the Resurrection of Jesus Christ is so overwhelming that it compels acceptance by proof, which leaves absolutely no room for doubt.[16]*

The signs and wonders in the Bible pertaining to the resurrection and other signs that Christ did were declared to be indisputable evidences because they were witnessed on the front lines. In 1 John 1:1-4, there is an abundant claim to the disciple's empirical observations surrounding the events of Christ's life:

> *That which was from the beginning, which we have heard, which we have seen with our eyes, which we looked upon and have touched with our hands, concerning the word of life—the life was made manifest, and we have seen it, and testify to it and proclaim to you the eternal life, which was with the Father and was made manifest to us—that which we have seen and heard we proclaim also to you, so that you too may have fellowship with us; and indeed our fellowship is with the Father and with his Son Jesus Christ. And we are writing these things so that our joy may be complete. (1 John 1:1-4)*

Notice the phrases, "we have heard," "we have seen with our eyes," "we have looked upon and have touched with our hands." The apostles were not superstitiously quick to believe in irrational concepts and tall tales, but were convinced through empirical evidence that Christ was indeed God through His life, speech, and even the miraculous events surrounding Him. They used both the experience of their senses and sound reason in order to try to convince others about the truth of what they knew, just as any rational person would do today. They saw it, they experienced it, they believed it, and they proclaimed it.

The Verdict

The time gap between the direct personal encounters that the disciples experienced and us is literally thousands of years. To many, this is the biggest issue that invites skepticism. This time gap is admittedly significant—but no more significant than any other trial case where a jury is separated from the events they are being called to judge. This is the nature of the court case.

What would our verdict be if we were on the panel of jurors for this case? We would first have to review the evidence. Let's look at what we have assessed so far.

If you will recall, our case is resting upon the proven reliability and trustworthiness of the Bible—a book that is unparalleled in its accuracy over that of any other ancient source. In it, we observed five eyewitness statements, four from the New Testament Gospels and one written later by Paul the apostle. These witness statements provided for us a timeline of the detailed events. We saw that there was no observable motive for lying about the resurrection, and their proclaiming of the resurrection message in dangerous places, where alienation and persecution provided a real threat, added to their sincerity. We also saw additional information from non-Christian sources, written years later, collaborating the claims circulating around the Jewish and Roman world, that Christ was believed by many to have risen from the dead.

If this case would be given in an earthly trial, the court's verdict would not be able to avoid the solid wall of historical evidence presented. The case for the resurrection is essentially a legally airtight case—it is a rational belief. From here, a rational person could easily conclude Christ indeed must have been raised from the dead from the evidence available. This conclusion best represents the evidence. Therefore, the historical resurrection ought to rest comfortably alongside every other ancient historical fact.

What Makes Christ's Divinity Convincing?

Allow me to play devil's advocate for just a moment. Does Jesus' mere verbal claim to divinity confirm that He actually was God? Not necessarily. Jesus made the claim to be God, but claims do not provide evidence for anything concrete. After all, other religious leaders have made similar incredible claims. We are not obligated to assume divinity to every person who claims divinity without any good evidence to support him or her in that claim.

What about the miracles He performed? Does the reality of Jesus performing miracles prove that Christ must have been God? Not really. Prophets have been able to accomplish similar types of signs under God's power. The performance of the miraculous could just indicate that God is at work by simply validating the ministry of a prophet.

What about what Jesus taught—were those teachings proof in any way of His divinity? No. The teachings of Jesus are not a sign that Jesus was God either, since many prophets and rabbis can be found throughout the ages to have taught with some similarity.

Lastly, what about the resurrection? Even the resurrection in and of itself doesn't confirm Christ's divine identity, because there are people in the Bible whom God has brought back from the dead—people who were not divine but subjected to the mercies of God through miraculous events.

So what then confirms Jesus Christ's divinity? Confirmation lies in a combination of both Jesus' claim to divinity, and the confirmation of those claims through the historical evidence of the miraculous—especially the resurrection. These two elements give us assurance that our faith is on firm ground.

The empty tomb was a supernatural signature of confirmation from the Father, approving Christ's earthly ministry—signaling to the world that God the Father was pleased with His Son. God would not raise a liar from the dead who spoke false things concerning God's name. If Jesus were a liar, then God could have easily just left Jesus in the tomb permanently, like every other man in history, and quickly make Him look like a scandalous fraud in the eyes of all who followed after Him.

It has now been demonstrated that the follower's faith can be rationally based upon a sound reflection of the evidence at hand—but is this the only evidence that is available? In fact, it is not—there is even greater evidence that supports the true identity of Jesus Christ—the objective signs of messianic prophecy.

7
The Prophetic Evidence
FOR JESUS CHRIST

God doesn't bride, child. He just makes a sign and lets people take it as they will.
STEPHEN KING, THE STAND

We have the prophetic word more fully confirmed, to which to which you will do well to pay attention as to a lamp shining in a dark place, until the day dawns and the morning star rises in your hearts, knowing this first of all, that no prophecy of scripture was ever produced by the will of man, but men spoke from God as they were carried along by the Holy Spirit.
2 PETER 1:19-21

I t was not only the miraculous events of Jesus' life that convinced His followers, both then and today, of His divine presence and authority. There was actually already a forceful undercurrent of messianic anticipation stirring in the hearts of the Israelites long before Christ was even born. Israel was expecting the scriptural promise of a prophet to replace Moses, a priest to replace Aaron, and a king to replace David. They were expecting the seed that was promised as far back as the Garden of Eden—the promise of a Messiah or "Anointed One."

Christ's fulfillment was a climax of long-awaited scriptural prophecies. The disciple Peter best uncovers the importance of this prophetic fulfillment. In 2 Peter 1:16-21, he writes:

> *For we did not follow* **cleverly devised myths** *when we made known to you the power and coming of our Lord Jesus Christ, but we were eyewitnesses of his majesty...And we have the prophetic word more fully confirmed...knowing this first of all, that no prophecy of Scripture comes from someone's own interpretation.* *For* **no prophecy was ever produced by the will of man, but men spoke from God as they were carried along by the Holy Spirit.**

Peter here expresses that many were eyewitnesses to the testimony of the resurrection, but in addition to the empirical evidence they already received, they were actually more *fully* confirmed in their belief of Christ through the "prophetic word."

We can readily trust the disciples' experiences due to analyzing the evidence previously provided, but with prophecy, even for those who weren't there to see Christ in the flesh, we can look to the Bible itself and objectively see Christ's messianic fulfillments, and become even more certain than those who were there at the time of Christ!

When we add the complete scripture and draw from the writings of the prophets who spoke God's decrees throughout the centuries, we see many prophecies that speak of a future day when a Messiah will come.

It is these scriptures concerning the coming Anointed One or "Christ" that we will now examine. Below is a list of some of the prophecies that communicate some of the events that were to happen in the life of the Messiah. Keep in mind that these prophecies were written hundreds of years before Christ.

Messianic Prophecies and Their Fulfillments

Prophecy 1: In Micah 5:2-5, the Messiah is claimed to be born in Bethlehem.

But you, O *Bethlehem* Ephrathah, who are too little to be among the clans of Judah, *from you shall come forth for me one who is to be ruler in Israel, whose coming forth is from of old, from ancient days.* Therefore he shall give them up until the time when she who is in labor has given birth; then the rest of his brothers shall return to the people of Israel. And he *shall stand and shepherd his flock in the strength of the Lord, in the majesty of the name of the Lord his God.* And they shall dwell secure, for now he shall be great to the ends of the earth. And he shall be their peace.

Fulfillment: Jesus Christ was indeed born in Bethlehem (Matthew 2:1-6):

Now after *Jesus was born in Bethlehem* of Judea in the days of Herod the king, behold, wise men from the east came to Jerusalem, saying, "Where is he who has been born king of the Jews? For we saw his star when it rose and have come to worship him." When Herod the king heard this, he was troubled, and all Jerusalem with him; and assembling all the chief priests and scribes of the people, he inquired of them where the Christ was to be born. They told him, "In Bethlehem of Judea, for so it is written by the prophet: 'And you, O Bethlehem, in the land of Judah, are by no means least among the rulers of Judah; for from you shall come a ruler who will shepherd my people Israel.'

Prophecy 2: The Messiah would be called Immanuel, which means, "God with us" (Isaiah 7:14).

> Therefore the Lord himself will give you a sign. Behold, the virgin shall conceive and bear a son, and shall *call his name Immanuel.*

Fulfillment: Jesus Christ is called Jesus or "Immanuel" (Matthew 1:21-23).

> She will bear a son, and you shall call his name Jesus, for he will save his people from their sins.' All this took place to fulfill what the Lord had spoken by the prophet: 'Behold, the virgin shall conceive and bear a son, and *they shall call his name Immanuel.*

Prophecy 3: The Messiah would be descended through the tribe of Judah (Genesis 49:10).

> *The scepter shall not depart from Judah,* nor the ruler's staff from between his feet, until tribute comes to him; and to *him shall be the obedience of the peoples.*

Fulfillment: Jesus' legal father Joseph was a descendent of David, who came from the line of Judah (Luke 3:23-33; Hebrews 7:14).

> Jesus, when he began his ministry, was about thirty years of age, being the son (as was supposed) of Joseph, the son of Heli...the son of Amminadab, the son of Admin, the son of Arni, the son of Hezron, the son of Perez, *the son of Judah* (Luke 3:23-33).

> Hebrews 7:14 says, "For it is evident that our Lord was descended *from Judah,* and in connection with that tribe Moses said nothing about priests."

Prophecy 4: A massacre of children would surround the Messiah's birth, as predicted in Jeremiah 31:15.

A voice is heard in Ramah, lamentation and bitter weeping. *Rachel is weeping for her children*; she refuses to be comforted for her children, because *they are no more.*

Fulfillment: Herod killed the infant children in Bethlehem, fearful that a prophesied king would be born and come to remove him from his throne (Matthew 2:16-18).

Then Herod, when he saw that he had been tricked by the wise men, became furious, and he sent and *killed all the male children in Bethlehem and in all that region who were two years old or under*, according to the time that he had ascertained from the wise men. Then was fulfilled what was spoken by the prophet Jeremiah: 'A voice was heard in Ramah, weeping and loud lamentation, Rachel weeping for her children; she refused to be comforted, because they are no more.'

The Prophecies of Isaiah

Out of all the prophecies found in the Bible involving the Messiah, it is in the book of Isaiah (written over seven hundred years before Christ was born) where we find the most staggering prophetic detail surrounding the suffering of the Messianic figure. I saved the best and most convincing proofs of Christ's identity as the divine Son of God for last.

Here in Isaiah 53:3-12, there are at least seventeen events and depictions that were fulfilled by Jesus Christ toward the end of His life. Let us now examine the infamous prophecy of Isaiah 53:3-12, starting in verse 3: "He was *despised and rejected by men; a man of sorrows*, and acquainted with grief; and as one from whom men hide their faces he was despised, and we esteemed him not."

155

- Christ was despised and rejected by men when His own people and disciple (Judas) delivered him over to the Romans for crucifixion. See Mark 14:41-42 and 15:15.

- Christ was identified as a man of sorrows, well acquainted with grief and weeping, throughout His ministry, even to the point of sweating drops of blood in mental sorrow and anguish. See Matthew 26:38, Mark 14:34, and Luke 22:45.

  Isaiah 53:4 tells us: "Surely he has bore our grief and carried our sorrows; yet we esteemed him stricken, smitten by God, and afflicted."

- Jesus Christ carried the burdens, pain and sins or "transgressions" of men in His suffering. See Luke 22:37.

  Verse 5 tells us: "But he was pierced for our transgressions; he was crushed for our iniquities; upon him was the chastisement that brought us peace, and with his wounds we are healed."

- Christ had a sacrificial plan or purpose in His suffering for the sins of others. See Acts 2:23-24.

- This sacrifice would bring peace and healing in the relationship between God and men. See Acts 3:17-21 and 17:26-27.

  Verse 6-7 tells us: "All we like sheep have gone astray; we have turned—every one—to his own way; and the Lord has laid on him the iniquity of us all. He was oppressed, and he was afflicted, yet he opened not his mouth; like a lamb that is led to the slaughter, and like a sheep that before its shearers is silent, so he opened not his mouth."

- Christ was judged and oppressed by others. See Matthew 26:57-59, 65-68 and Luke 23:20-25.

- Jesus Christ was persecuted but did not open His mouth to defend Himself. See Matthew 26:62-63.

  Verse 8 tells us: "By oppression and judgment he was taken away; and as for his generation, who considered that *he was cut off out of the land of the living*, stricken for the transgression of my people?"

- Christ died by crucifixion. See Mark 15:37, 43-44 and John 19:30-34.

  Verse 9 tells us: "And *they made his grave with the wicked* and with a rich man in his death, although he had done no violence, and there was *no deceit in his mouth*."

- Jesus died a common Roman criminal's death—death upon the cross. See Matthew 27:44 and John 19:18.

- Christ was buried with a rich man in His death. See Matthew 27:57-60.

- Christ's reputation was a sinless one, marked without any violence or deceit. See Matthew 26:59-60, 27:22-23 and Mark 14:55-59.

  Verse 10 tells us: "Yet *it was the will of the Lord to crush him*; he has put him to grief; when his soul makes an offering for guilt, he shall see his offspring; he shall prolong his days; the *will of the Lord shall prosper in his hand*."

- The cross was God's will for His Son Jesus, to be wounded for the sins of many. See Matthew 26:39 and Acts 2:23.

- Christ was to be a guilt offering on our behalf. See Hebrews 10:11-18.

- By the will of the Lord, our devotion and obedience shall prosper. See Acts 2:42-47 and 3:26.

  Verse 11 tells us: "Out of the anguish of his soul he shall see and be satisfied; by his knowledge shall the righteous one, my servant, *make many to be accounted righteous,* and he shall bear their iniquities."

- Because of Jesus, God will count many to be righteous (in good standing with God) before His eyes. See Acts 10:36-43.

Verse 12 tells us: "Therefore I will divide him a portion with the many, and he shall divide the spoil with the strong, because he poured out his soul to death and was numbered with the transgressors; yet *he bore the sin of many, and makes intercession for the transgressors.*"

- Jesus intercedes (petitions God the Father in prayer) for His believers. See John 17:1-26.

Prophetic Probability

It's important to remember that all of the prophecies Isaiah wrote were written about seven hundred years before the time of Christ's birth. This timeframe renders it impossible for Jesus to have orchestrated all the prophetic predictions found in Isaiah. This is especially true with regard to the independent actions of His enemies, political conditions of His time, and even the circumstances surrounding His foretold birth that is documented in other places in the Bible as well. These are very specific prophecies that could not be staged.

In working with these prophecies and many others, the mathematician Peter W. Stoner, using the *science of probability,* has calculated that the odds of one man fulfilling just sixteen of these messianic prophecies as 1 in 10^{45} power (1 in $10^{\,000\,000\,000\,000\,000\,000\,000\,000\,000\,000\,000\,000\,000\,000\,000}$), which is a staggeringly unfathomable number. In order to visualize this incredible number, Mr. Stoner illustrates:

Take this number of silver dollars. If you make these into a solid ball, you will have a great sphere with a center at the earth, and extending in all directions more than 30 times as far as from the earth to the sun. (If a train had started from the earth at the time the Declaration of Independence was signed, and had traveled steadily toward the sun at the rate of sixty miles per hour, day and night, it would be about reaching its destination today. But remember that our ball of silver dollars extends thirty times that far in all directions.) If you can imagine the marking of one silver dollar, and then thoroughly stirring it into this great ball, and blindfolding a man and telling him to pick out one dollar, and expect it to be the marked one, you have somewhat of a picture of how absolutely the fulfillment of sixteen prophecies referring to Jesus Christ proves both that He is the Son of God and that our Bible is inspired. Certainly God directed the writing of His Word.[17]

But Stoner continues adding more messianic prophecies into that equation for a sum total of 48 messianic prophecies. He concludes that the odds of one man fulfilling 48 of these messianic prophecies are an astonishing 1 in 10^{157}! This number is actually impossible to comprehend, giving us no room to doubt the fact that Jesus Christ was indeed the Jewish Messiah and the foretold Savior of the world. It is therefore unquestionably rational for anyone to conclude with this mathematical probability that, according to the scriptures, Jesus alone qualifies to be the Messiah.

In fact, opposing this conclusion of Christ's messianic destiny and accomplishments would be to cling to an impossible counter fact that needs justification. When considering these odds, *it is actually impossible that Jesus could not have been the Messiah, the Son of God.* Therefore, we too must conclude with Professor Stoner that, "Any man who rejects Christ as the Son of God is rejecting a fact proved perhaps more absolutely than any other fact in the world."[18]

Even if the evidence for both the resurrection and prophecy were the only two arguments for God's existence (excluding all-natural arguments presented earlier), then a Christian still has the rational upper hand.

When you see such a clear fulfillment of numerous prophecies in the Old Testament (which was written centuries before the birth of Jesus), reason is quick to admit that the inter-time sign of prophecy is something that only God could ever bring about. The probability is far too high for it not to be something divine. Likewise, when you see such clear historical evidence for the resurrection, reason again must admit that God accomplished this, since any power over death and new life are in divine hands alone. Now add both of these miraculous things together. This brings me to conclude that if Jesus says that He is the Son of God, then I will wholeheartedly believe Him based off His works, just as He asked us to believe. And quite frankly, anything else He says needs to be paid attention to as well.

Faith in Christ, for the Christian, is therefore not an irrational, subjective jump into a blind absurdity, but a logical trust and reliance upon the facts that sufficiently support Christ. After all, I highly doubt that God would resurrect and thus confirm the ministry of someone who is a liar and deceives others in the name of God—obviously the Jesus who was resurrected by God's all-powerful hand must be of the Truth.

Conclusion

So far, we have concluded that there is a maximally great Intellect behind the universe's existence. He is the one that has left the traceability of His fingerprints upon the grand display of the colossal stars of the galaxies, down to the most infinitesimal micro-designs of our quantum world.

This Uncaused Personal Mind has not only left traces of His existence scattered throughout the created order of things but loved us enough to communicate to us directly. This Uncaused Mind communicated to us by written words through the holy Bible, as recorded by the Hebrew people through their prophets, priests, apostles and delegates. The claims of divine inspiration as found in scripture and the claim of Jesus Christ supports all that we could expect of God in communicating to us—a claim to divinity (the first criterion) and the validating of those claims through the miraculous proofs (our second criterion).

In the cumulative case of all that has been presented thus far, a rational person may trust in Jesus Christ and His word without any sort of "religious crutch", or attachment to blind faith. The Christian faith has always been the faith where rational people can concur with the truths of reality and experience without committing intellectual suicide. Accepting the worldview is good, intellectually speaking, God desires to deliver a particular message—this is the whole purpose in His communication to us in the first place. This revelation is what we will deal with next, in our efforts to understand more about who this God truly is and what He finds so important as to write to us about.

8
God's Message
Part 1:
THE TERRIBLE NEWS

*God exists whether or not men may choose to believe in Him. The reason
why many people do not believe in God is not so much that it is intellectually
impossible to believe in God, but because belief in God forces that thoughtful
person to face the fact that he is accountable to such a God.*

ROBERT A. LAIDLAW

'None is righteous, no, not one;
no one understands;
no one seeks for God.
All have turned aside; together they have become worthless;
no one does good,
not even one.'

ROMANS 3:9-12

The historical and natural accuracies, the miraculous
resurrection event, and the supernatural prophetic evidences of scripture and Christ ought to scream to our
minds that the Bible is what it has always claimed to be—the

declarations of God. Since God has revealed Himself in a reliable way throughout the ancient Hebrew texts of the Old Testament and the writings of the New Testament, we are now free to learn and absorb all that we can about what God teaches us.

Our calling is to thoroughly study God's Word so that we might know God and dedicate our lives to His faithful service in love, hope, and humility—in the way that He desires, not our own opinions. What we ought to be asking ourselves at this point is "What is the essence—the central message—of God's Word?" According to God, what is the most important information that I could ever know?

Thankfully, this message is repeated and illustrated all over the Bible, in many different ways. Its thread is found woven throughout the poetic, historical, and prophetic books, and centralizes itself within the Gospel accounts. This message is in fact called "The Gospel."

The term gospel means "good news," and because this is God's focus in His book, it will be the main focus for the remainder of this book. But first, in order to understand how our Creator's Gospel is actually good news, we must first understand what the bad news is. Only then will we truly understand, embrace, and benefit from the Gospel news.

The Terrible News

The first element of the bad news is that sin entered into creation through human disobedience. When God created the contingent universe, He did so flawlessly, according to the ways of His good and perfect character. In His perfection, God formed man out of the Earth and placed within him a living soul. Genesis 2:7 reveals to us that "the Lord God formed the man of dust from the ground and breathed into his nostrils the breath of life, and the man became a living creature."

Adam and Eve were beautifully and wonderfully formed with the divine image imprinted into their human nature. Genesis 1:27 states: "God created man in his own image, in the image of God he created him; male and female he created them." Adam and Eve were adequately prepared with qualities that reflected God's character and personal attributes, just as we spoke about at the beginning of Part 1 in this book. Their ethics, reason, intellect, free will, consciousness, artistic creativity, and self-awareness all demonstrated the image-bearing differences that were distinct from the other animals in creation. Mankind outweighed the glory of any other beast that the Lord God made.

They would continue to dwell in the paradise of Eden that God provided for them—unscathed by death, evil, or pain. While in this perpetual state, the rest of the created world would be set up for man to dominate in faithful stewardship. In the garden, God provided every tree for food, seeds for nutrients, fruit for pleasure and lasting life, animals for company, and each other for companionship. God gave them everything and lavished His kindness and goodness upon them at the beginning.

In the midst of all these wonderful things, God issued a single warning for Adam and Eve—do not touch the fruit from the tree of the "Knowledge of Good and Evil". For reasons that God alone possesses, He saw fit to provide an option for Adam and Eve to freely reject His presence and blessing if they so desired. By obeying—they would express their love and contentment toward God, acknowledging His authority over them. Through rebellion, they would declare their independence from God, revealing their lack of love and discontentment with His grace. God clearly desired that Adam and Eve would be not ignorant of the lasting consequences of such a choice and so fairly and plainly warned them of the penalty that would come with that choice—death.

It wasn't too long after this that the first man and woman broke this command and committed cosmic treason against God (Genesis 3:1-13). Because of their temptation and allowing themselves to be willfully deceived through the lead of Satan, they led themselves and all of their descendants into a sin-stricken nature.

From this willful disobedience, the curse of sin became a part of man's nature—a darkened, naturally selfish instinct ingrained into our character, our will, and our heart's pleasures. Like a hereditary flesh-eating disease, sin has been passed down to us from our original parents, along with all of its physically and spiritually disabling effects. This is what we see when we see a beautiful and orderly world contaminated with noticeable imperfections and selfish cruelty—we see the effects of sin. The Bible calls this "The Curse."

All people agree that the world just doesn't *seem* right—that things aren't what they *ought* to be. We know through an inner instinct in our souls that things are wrong with the world, generally and with us specifically. There is no religion that doesn't recognize this; there is no philosophy or political ideology that omits the fact that there are problems in this world, which are in need of fixing—they just disagree on how to fix it.

Our once fruitful and innocent life in Adam is now darkened and tainted. Because of "The Fall," all people are now currently separated from the perfect and holy God who created them. In this state, God has mercifully set a time limit on us—death. God cannot be in the presence of sin and will not tolerate sin to exist forever in His creation, so God separated Himself from Adam and Eve by casting them out of the Garden of Eden and announced that the descendants of Adam shall inevitably die.

"It is appointed for man to die once, and after that comes judgment" (Hebrews 9:27).

Even though Adam and Eve were cast out, they were not without hope. God declared that an offspring would one day come from the descendants of Adam and Eve, who would crush the head of Satan after being bruised by him (Genesis 3:15). This is the first hint of the good news that is to come.

Our God is Righteous and Just

The second aspect of the bad news is found within the perfect nature of God Himself. God is good, just, and perfect—this is bad news for you and me! This might sound strange—that God being good is somehow bad news. It's bad in the sense that if God is good, just, and perfect in all of His actions, then His judgments will be precise and accurate toward every individual person, without any favoritism, as He announces His verdict toward us on Judgment Day. This includes you.

Every widow who has ever been ripped off by a crook, every child or adult who has ever been physically or sexually abused, every poor or elderly person who has been unjustly treated or taken advantage of can be comforted that the all-seeing, all-knowing God is aware of their situation. He is the Avenger of the weak and defenseless. Vengeance is delivered daily from His hand upon the wicked and evil men who oppress others and boast in their wickedness. God often causes the sins that men plan to do to others to fall upon themselves in *earthly* justice, but God will make all things just *eternally* speaking as well.

This attribute of pure justice is an attractive aspect of God's character, especially for those who have been oppressed. You only need to read through the newspaper once to be convinced that we lack a perfect justice system. We desire a system that will competently dispense flawless justice in a way no earthly court could ever hope to accomplish. Our God *has* this power, and He *will* exercise it.

Unfortunately, this wonderful attribute of God's nature is actually everyone's worst enemy—this is *your* worst enemy. Not only must God judge the horrible actions of history—national genocide, serial murders, tyranny, and ghastly acts of warfare—but divine justice will flow like a flood downward upon the more "acceptable sins" of the common person. Sin is any violation of His law and our conscience, no matter what form it takes—inevitably, all will confess it in His throne room one day. Willful sins such as lying, selfishness, greed, theft, hatred, bitterness, anger, violence, abusiveness, sexual immorality, slander, and gossip must be dealt with by God.

Think about it. Most will agree that God (if He is good by nature) must bring punishment to this world's evils. But then, we must consistently consider also our own evil in the same way, knowing that God will also secure justice for the people that we have hurt as well. God does not show partiality or favoritism; He must punish sin wherever it is found. Nahum 1:3 says, "the Lord will by no means clear the guilty." If we acknowledge that God will punish the most notorious of guilty criminals, then we must too be consistent coming to terms with our own guilt and punishment as well.

If you are anything like me, then you too, have committed serious wrongs against others. God is fair, for the scripture states that "God will bring every deed into judgment, with every secret thing, whether good or evil" (Ecclesiastes 12:14). Furthermore, we must know that "no creature is hidden from his sight, but all are naked and exposed to the eyes of him to whom we must give account" (Hebrews 4:13).

We Are Exposed

The third aspect of the bad news is that our sin is exposed in the light of Christ. Some might ask, "How do I know that I have sinned?" The answer is through your conscience. Romans 2:14-15 reveals:

> For when Gentiles, who do not have the law, by nature do what the law requires, they are a law to themselves, even though they do not have the law. They show that **the work of the law is written on their hearts, while their conscience also bears witness, and their conflicting thoughts accuse or even excuse them.**

God has given us His laws written upon the tablets of our conscience to be our moral guide. When we violate these moral laws, we feel conflicted in our thoughts and they accuse us of our wrong, even if we choose to ignore and suppress them. God has also revealed to the nation of Israel a set of laws— the famous Ten Commandments—that reflect God's holy and moral character even further. Since the word *sin* technically means "to miss the mark" of God's standard for perfection, the law of God then acts as a practical mirror that reflects our shortcomings from God's standard. This is how we know what sin is. With both our conscience and the law of God, we can look to see whether we are truly "good people" according to God's standard.

I know this is heavy and your heart might be sinking, but we must continue in the bad news a bit further so the good news will be made all the sweeter. Let's look at some personal examples of how we fall short of God's standard for righteousness.

One of the Ten Commandments says "You shall not murder." Jesus likewise expanded upon this commandment by saying:

*You have heard that it was said to those of old, 'You shall not murder; and whoever murders shall be liable to judgment.' But I say to you that everyone who is **angry with his brother** will be liable for judgment; whoever **insults his brother** will be liable to the council; and whoever says, 'You fool!' will be liable to the hell of fire"* (Matthew 5:21-22).

Have you ever hated another person? Shouted names at someone in anger or abusive rage behind the wheel of your vehicle? Jesus called this murder of the heart, and it is worthy of judgment.

We could continue through each one of these commandments and find ourselves sinking deeper and deeper into guilt—this is only one commandment of ten! We could also ask if we have ever pushed God back from first in our lives, stolen (including movies and music off the internet), dishonored our parents in our speech or rebellion, desired things that were someone else's, and so on. All of us have both directly and indirectly failed in thousands, even millions of ways against the two major commands of scripture—to love God with all our heart, soul, mind, and strength; and secondly, to love our neighbor as we love ourselves.

I think you get the point regarding this aspect of the terrible news—we are all going to be standing guilty before a holy, just God for our mountainous stacks of sin.

Common Excuses on Judgment Day

At this point, many tend to say or think of excuses in order to soften their stinging conscience and ease the thoughts of their sobering position before God. This is an especially dangerous self-delusion that will keep people in denial of the eternal consequences of their sin—passing off the thought until it's too late, and they must stand before God. Some are prepared to go through life and bank their eternity on a few excuses that would never be acceptable in any earthly court system, but somehow think that it will work in God's heavenly courtroom.

Many might say to God, "But God, I may have done some bad things, but I'm mostly a good person." How long would it last in an earthly court case? Image you murdered someone, and you stood before the judge and jury saying, "Yeah, I murdered that person, but I'm mostly a good person." What would that judge say to you? The judge wouldn't care about any supposed goodness that you claim to possess. Good deeds do not buy people immunity from evil crimes. It is the crime that must be punished and dealt with—any other good deeds that you had accumulated in your life are completely irrelevant to the laws that have been broken.

In an attempt to escape the justice of God, someone might also say, "Look, I know that I have sinned, but I have since stopped doing these things." Again, if we took that excuse before a local judge, what would be the reply to you, the murderer? I'm sure He would be glad that you stopped murdering, but you must stand trial for the murder that you have already committed. So it is with us; our judge is sentencing us for what we have done—your current lifestyle choices are irrelevant. The penalty must be paid for the crime committed.

I could see someone also attempting to plea, "But God is a loving and forgiving God. He would never do that!" A loving and forgiving God He is, but His love and forgiveness are just as important as His justice, which all must perfectly exist together and not impose upon the other's requirements.

Finally, a person might lean on their religious deeds to escape punishment. Standing before God they might say, "But

I read my Bible every day, been baptized, confessed my sin, go to church every Sunday, make my tithe, etc." If this defense was given to any justice system on the planet, the response would be the same as the person who thinks themselves to be a good person, only now they are trying to use religious works as a credit or way of escape.

If these excuses cannot carry weight in the faulty justice systems of Earth, we can be certain that they will definitely not be of warrant in God's heavenly courtroom. The qualifications that judges on Earth lack in order to establish perfect justice is the ability to possess all the knowledge relevant to the case, access to the criminal's inner-heart motives, and an unbiased soul. All of these things God alone possesses, making His justice flawless, flushing out any of our vain attempts to hide our guilt.

Hell: God's Place of Torment

The last portion of the terrible news is that *if God were to give us what we logically, truly and justly deserve, then we would end up with some form of punishment. God calls that punishment "Hell."* Judgment Day is coming when everyone will be brought to God for our final eternal placement—Heaven or Hell.

If we are honest, we must admit that we are guilty of violating our conscience and breaking God's moral laws hundreds of thousands of times within our lifetime. So just as a criminal must pay the consequences of his lawlessness in jail (regardless of his intention), we too must face our mountainous stack of charges in Hell forever.

In the classic allegory Dante's *Inferno*, Dante and his companion Virgil tour Hell, where they witness a terrifying phrase above the gates of Hell, "*Abandon all hope, ye who enter here.*" The point made is that if you die in your sin after a life of rejecting God, this statement will certainly be true of your state.

How then could we ever get right with God? To this answer we now thankfully turn.

9
God's Message Part 2:
THE GOOD NEWS

No scene in sacred history ever gladdens the soul like the scene on Calvary.
CHARLES SPURGEON

God shows his love for us in that while we were still sinners,
Christ died for us.
ROMANS 5:8

Despite our condition, we can be thankful that God, in His infinite wisdom, foresaw our dire need for help and predestined a solution that has come to pass. God, in His rich mercy and love, has a plan that honors and exercises both His just and gracious nature through the accomplishment of a plan of salvation or deliverance.

This plan of *salvation* or *deliverance* from sin is what the entire Bible is all about—this is God's message to mankind. It could be summed up in the famous John 3:16 passage. John writes in verses 16 and 17: "For God so loved the world, that he gave his only Son, that whoever believes in him should not perish but have eternal life. For God did not send his Son into the world to condemn the world, but in order that the world might be saved through him."

God sent His Son Jesus Christ to live and die in the place of the sinner as the sacrificial payment for their sin. Jesus willingly chose to die on the cross for the sins of many, taking on the full punishment of God that they should receive. He also rose again from the grave on the third day, showing us that Christ is who He claimed to be, that death is both conquered by Christ and a thing of the past for those in Christ.

In this cross, God maintained His responsibility to accomplish justice, and yet, through this plan, is able to show His love and mercy at the same time, by pardoning all who call upon the name Jesus Christ. Jesus said of Himself in John 14:6 that "I am the way, and the truth, and the life. No one comes to the Father except through me." He alone is our hope to conquer the effects of sin, reunite us with our God, and give us eternal life again. He alone overturns the curse of the terrible news and replaces it with the promised blessing of Heaven.

Imagine yourself as a criminal who has been placed in chains and led into a courtroom to stand before the noblest and fairest judge in the country. The fine that you owe for your crime is an amount too large for you to ever hope to pay, so you stand, anxiously and hopelessly awaiting your sentence.

But as you wait for your sentence to be handed down, a mysterious man suddenly enters the courtroom and asks the judge if he can pay the court the money required for your crimes so that you may be completely pardoned of every charge—the judge accepts the offer and sets you free from the penalty. How wonderfully relieving would that be?! The judge's main concern for the payment has been satisfied—justice has been faithfully administered at the cost of the stranger. The penalty is paid, the chains are removed—you are now free!

Now imagine this same scenario but upon a far grander scale—this legal transaction is what Christ accomplished for sinners. No one could dare to question the power of such a love that this stranger has shown toward you in that he would sacrifice himself (though he was innocent of any crime) and willingly take your guilt upon himself to set you free from your offences. Romans 5:6-8 declares:

> For while we were still weak, at the right time Christ died for the ungodly. For one will scarcely die for a righteous person—though perhaps for a good person one would dare even to die—but God shows his love for us in that while we were still sinners, Christ died for us.

How Are We Then Saved?

So how is it that we can receive this payment for our sin? How can we be delivered from the penalty of sin and satisfy God's justice?

This happens when you embrace Jesus Christ as the Messiah God promised to mankind in His scriptures. *Your hope for eternal life is solely found in Christ and nothing else. This is because it is His cross alone that provides the legal payment that makes it possible for God to forgive all of your sin.* In embracing Christ by faith alone, you will be considered justified before God and His heavenly court case against you will forever be dismissed. The only payment that God will ever accept for sin hangs there on the cross of Calvary for you to humbly and freely receive. At the point of faith in Christ, your relationship with God changes. The very God that was once your Judge is now satisfied through Christ, and now through faith becomes your delighted and loving Father, who eagerly welcomes you into His family through adoption. Colossians 2:13-14 speaks of this when it says:

> And you, who were dead in your trespasses...God made alive together with him, having forgiven us all our trespasses, by canceling the record of debt that stood against us with its legal demands. This he set aside, nailing it to the cross.

It will be through Christ's perfect, sinless life imparted to you that you will possess the righteousness that God will credit into your spiritual bank account, so to speak. It will be through the historical fact of Christ's resurrection from the tomb that your promised hope for future life and your victory over death will be obtained. Everything that God has promised is received by giving your life over to Him. Our debts and records of sin are then completely washed away—past, present, and future— all because of the accomplishments of Christ. In this way, when we die, we will stand favorably before God; it will not be because of our favor or good deeds, but because of the shed blood of Jesus on our behalf.

God will get all the glory for solving our sin problem, not us— we just receive it by faith. We ourselves could never be saved, so God took that initiative upon Himself in love to do it for us!

The Grace of God

God saves us by grace, a word that means "undeserved love and favor from God." The Bible says that salvation is an act of God working in us, according to His will. God provided you the sorrow for your sin; God made a way for the Gospel to come to you that you might hear it (perhaps through this book), and God draws a person to Himself in order to provide the gift of faith, that you might receive it and trust in Christ's work. From the beginning of your faith journey until the very end, God is the Author of your salvation and works in you to accomplish His will. Ephesians 2:8-9 lays out the nature of our salvation well: "For by grace you have been saved through faith. And this is not your own doing; it is the gift of God, not a result of works, so that no one may boast." Because of the role grace plays in a person coming to Christ, we must forget about any attempts to earn God's favor through baptism, church attendance, or any other list of "good deeds." Instead, we must rest only upon Christ's finished works and the grace of God working in us, who has so moved and caused us to receive Him. All the credit goes to God.

There will be no bragging about our own goodness when we stand before God. No one will be able to bring a spiritual report card before God and declare that they ought to be let into God's presence because of a misguided sense of personal worthiness. The only thing that will be acceptable to God on Judgment Day will be the fact that we have humbly admitted our unworthiness to God and turned to Christ. It is the report card of Christ that is worthy in God's sight and it is offered to us by relying on Him.

At the cross, justice can be satisfied and mercy administered to us. Sin can be removed, enabling divine forgiveness to take place. God will not look upon our sin anymore; instead, He will see the righteousness of His Son in its place.

The Righteousness of Jesus for Us

What do I mean when I say that the righteousness of Christ is in our bank account? Allow me to explain.

Jesus' purpose was to obey perfectly every command of God for our sake. He obeyed God in an active sense by following all the laws that God gave to Israel, and He also entrusted all circumstances and situations into the hands of the Father in a passive sense. Jesus literally fulfilled God's will perfectly, and by doing this, He carried out His mission in fulfilling everything that is righteous in God's eyes.

He did this because, from Adam onwards, no human could keep from disobeying God and falling into some form of sin that will eventually carry a punishment. So Christ literally lived the perfect life that we could not, facing the same types of temptation and challenges that we have faced, but instead of falling *into* them, Jesus obeyed God perfectly *through* them. He conquered all temptation and never gave way to sin in any shape or form.

Christ's life is the perfect template of what an obedient human life looks like in God's sight. This was done in order that He might give this righteousness to us. We could say that, by faith, not only does our sin get put onto Christ's shoulders in order to bear the anger of God for us, but also that His "alien" righteousness gets put onto us in order to experience God's favor and blessing. 2 Corinthians 5:21 says, "For our sake he made him to be sin who knew no sin, so that *in him we might become the righteousness of God.*" It is a spiritual transaction or *substitution* that occurs in Jesus—all sin is removed from you and is punished on the cross, and all of Christ's righteousness is infused into you, making you acceptable in God's sight!

The Victory of the Resurrection

The spiritual and physical significance of the resurrection is that, in Christ's resurrected life, He has shown that He reigns over the process of death. God provides a promise to those who trust in His Son, that they will be resurrected just as Jesus was resurrected—made anew in a glorified body. Death for the child of God is therefore only a slight, yet necessary, inconvenience to transition us from one place (Earth) to another (Heaven).

This is why the cross is so significant; it is here that the most ashamed or sinful people are able to find themselves united with their Creator. No matter your gender, nationality, social standing, financial worth, dark past—or any other obstacle that you could imagine—God can absolve you of your sin, permanently striking all from the record and creating you sinless and new in the future resurrection of the dead.

God will never turn away from a man, woman, or child who comes to Him. All who come to Christ will be united eternally and physically with their estranged Creator and enjoy His eternal delights in the resurrection, as Revelation 21:1-6 foretells:

Then I saw a new heaven and a new earth, for the first heaven and the first earth had passed away, and the sea was no more. And I saw the holy city, new Jerusalem, coming down out of heaven from God, prepared as a bride adorned for her husband. And I heard a loud voice from the throne saying, 'Behold, the dwelling place of God is with man. He will dwell with them, and they will be his people, and God himself will be with them as their God. He will wipe away every tear from their eyes, and death shall be no more, neither shall there be mourning, nor crying, nor pain anymore, for the former things have passed away.' And he who was seated on the throne said, 'Behold, I am making all things new.' Also he said, 'Write this down, for these words are trustworthy and true.

True Faith versus Hypocritical Faith

So is that it? As long as I have faith in Christ, I can go on living a life of sin and not worry about anything? No. The faith that allows cooperation with a life of sin is no true biblical faith in any sense—it is a shallow, hypocritical, and superficial replacement. True faith in Christ is a living organism, so to speak. Those who are saved by God live their lives by that faith and live in a continuous state of repentance.

Repentance implies two things: firstly, it is a *desire that accompanies faith in desperately attempting to turn from the same sin* that put our Savior on the cross in the first place. Sins such as deceitfulness, injustice, selfish desires, immorality, anger, coarse and perverted speech, addictive habits, and all other forms of sinful practices associated with your current life must first be recognized. Then, upon a deeper understanding of God's felt position on these things, you turn from them and adopt God's view on the matter. This is the essence of repentance—turning away from sin and towards God.

Secondly, while repentance means to turn away from sin, it also implies that we will *turn toward something else*: God. When we turn from sin, we cannot just stop sinning; we must also replace those sinful habits by turning to all that is pleasurable in God's sight. The Holy Spirit of God will aid us in weeding out of sins from our garden of the soul.

What is the Evidence of Salvation?

How then do you know if God has indeed saved you? I think I am trusting in Jesus Christ for my forgiveness, but how do I know for sure that it's genuine? As I mentioned, God initially saves us by His grace through faith. When you recognize your sins and trust wholly in Jesus and His sacrifice, you are saved once and for all.

God also saves us in a *continuous* sense through the lifelong process of change, called *sanctification*, which takes place in the soul of every believer. In this sense, a person is being saved continuously by growing more and more in obedience to God in every area of life, experiencing an ever-growing conviction of sin, developing a deeper sensitivity of conscience, increasing in the understanding of Christ, and developing a desire to read the Bible, to live in good will toward others, and to pray. All this is actively at work due to the Spirit of God creating in you a fresh, God-thirsty soul. It is an active grace of God working in you to change and guide you into holiness—into becoming like Jesus.

So how will we know that we have been truly saved and are still being saved? The answer is simple: through the inner and outer witness of the Holy Spirit producing in you a growing love for Christ, a strong love for brothers and sisters in Christ (the church), a love for your neighbors, a love for your enemies, and a love for the things of God.

If there has not been a renewal of your *old* nature into a *new* creature of love toward God and others, then cry out to God in prayer day and night until He noticeably accomplishes this work within your soul. This is the substance of our final complementary piece of evidence in the next chapter—the evidence of a life transformed by God.

10
A Final Piece of Evidence:
MY TESTIMONY

Therefore if anyone is in Christ he is a new creation. The old has passed away; behold, the new has come...Therefore we are ambassadors for Christ, God making His appeal through us. We implore you on behalf of Christ, be reconciled to God.

2 Corinthians 5:17, 20

The Christian's biblical worldview is also experiential—which is why I must not forget to include my own personal experiences with God as a further testament to His glory. The problem with this type of argument is that it is highly subjective. Even still, just as the apostle's post-resurrection experiences with Christ provided powerful evidence for the resurrection, so too there are incredible encounters with God—that if true—are further evidence supporting a God who continues to reveal Himself today. Experiences can be misinterpreted, misunderstood, and just plain wrong, but do all of them fall into these categories? I think not.

My testimony won't be convincing to many, but nevertheless is a personal truth that I was involved in, and so it too must be offered in defense of the glory of God and the rationality of the Christian faith. Experience is one of the most convincing proofs for individuals, but at the same time, the least impressive for those outside of those experiences. This is simply because the experience cannot be replicated or verified by anyone expect the person or persons involved—skepticism is natural but the testimony is irrefutable if truly interpreted.

What do I mean by personal experiences? Personal experiences such as responses to specific prayer and perfectly-timed acts of providence are some such experiences that powerfully point to the divine. So powerful are these experiences that people will remain unmovable, even if someone could dismantle all other forms of scientific and historical argument. Someone could have the Bible supposedly disproven, natural revelations explained away—and yet, because of their personal experience with the Living God, remain unwavering in their commitments to Christ and His word. They remain unmoved because they experienced Him first-hand and know better than to doubt Him.

For example, I can tell you without a doubt that I had green tea at lunch today. This experience that I am claiming provides no way for you to ultimately test to see if I am telling you the truth or not. You would simply have to believe my subjective testimony of it. By the time you read this, so much time would have passed that any evidence that now exists in my house (old tea leaves in the compost, dirty cup by the sink) will be long gone and unable to be tested. Yet, I am certain of this tea experience, even if you can't verify it. I know that it is true, even without your approval of this fact.

Let's say you are somehow strangely opposed to the idea that I had this cup of tea this morning—you think it never happened. You might be able to convince me of the unlikelihood that it was tea I had or attempt to argue that it was all just a dream. You might stack logical evidences and well-thought out objections, but regardless of my inability to answer you logically or properly, I am still ultimately correct on my own experience, regardless of whether I can compete with you through argumentation.

In a similar fashion, a person can still be rational when it comes down to even subjective experiences, so long as it is correctly interpreted, and logical conclusions support it. We could be skeptical about all the "intellectual" arguments used thus far in this book and yet be most assured—beyond a shadow of any doubt—that the Christian faith is true.

My Witness Testimony

Allow me to now share my own personal experience that helped me to solidify my conviction of the Christian faith—this is my legal testimony. Before I became a Christian on January 23, 2006, I was a militant atheist. I had sought on many occasions to brashly liberate Christian people from the organized religious crutches of the Christian faith. God was to me a Santa Claus-type fairy tale that adults had invented in order to cope with the heartache of death and suffering—a tool to remain optimistic in a purposeless life. I believed that men invented the concept of God as an abusive tool to prey upon poor, unintelligent, weak, and gullible people.

As I was then, so I am now—a realist driven by a desire for truth, not blind faith or subjective emotional appeals. By God's grace, I was personally committed to truth, and if a religion was not based upon truthful claims but upon fantasy, then it must be an ideology to fight against—because no matter how much "good" it does, it is *still* a lie.

It was during 2004 and 2005 that I began to notice that a few friends of mine had become Christians, so I engaged in friendly debates to challenge their beliefs. I propelled arguments against them such as: where are the evidences for God? Why would a loving God send people to Hell? Why would God allow for evil and suffering? Evolution is a proven fact, so how can you believe in the Bible and the six-day creation account?

I noticed that many of my Christians friends were unable to answer my questions, and so I thought that they haven't given much thought to their own faith system. This ignorance of their own beliefs only confirmed my conviction that the idea of God was an imaginative invention. This blind faith infuriated me! I couldn't comprehend how people could just believe something without thinking deeply about it or, at the very least, asking questions to examine what they were being told. It seemed to me to be a very emotional decision without any realistic grounds.

I started reading the Bible with the aim of finding the particular story that I had heard, where God had ordered Israel to kill Canaanites in the Promised Land. I planned to use this scripture as a reference to show my friends the questionable nature of this "loving" God in whom they believed.

I had reached Deuteronomy 4:29, when I found this passage: "But from there you will seek the Lord your God, and you will find Him if you search for Him with all your heart and all your soul."

This particular verse gripped me; it was an intriguing statement—I saw it at the time as an invitation for me to challenge the God of this book who claimed to be able to reveal Himself. So right then, that night, in my room, I did just that. For the first time ever, I prayed to the God of the Hebrews. My prayer was more of a mockery saying, "God, if you are real, then reveal

Yourself to me. If You are able to show yourself to Moses and the Israelites, then it shouldn't be a problem for You to show yourself to little ol' me." I expected nothing to happen and to continue on with my life from there. At least I was settled in my soul, could say to myself that I had tried prayer, and could then tell my friends that their belief was bogus—prayer doesn't work either.

As a background, up until that point (aside from an odd experience I had with an Ouija board when I was younger), I had not even the slightest belief in the supernatural, since there were no reasons for me to justify believing in anything outside of a natural account of the world. My worldview exactly matched what the public school system had indoctrinated me to believe—a naturalistic, materialistic, humanistic philosophy.

After I prayed, however, odd things began to happen. I experienced numerous strange and—what I considered to be—unnatural occurrences all around me over the span of a few months. I recall one occasion when I was having a conversation about the person of Christ at a person's house. During our conversation, lights began to flicker on and off. We were within eyesight of the light switch, and no one else was with us in the room—a strange phenomenon that I had never experienced before and haven't since. Other strange happenings occurred, but I stubbornly classified all such incidents as mere coincidences and filed them away in the back of my mind.

Finally, one of my friends (we will call her Rachel) called to tell me that her mother, who wasn't a Christian at the time, had been healed when a pastor prayed for her at a local church. I was already aware that she had experienced bad leg pain for a long time, which required frequent use of medications. Being my skeptical self, I didn't believe that she had been healed until I visited her home and saw it for myself. Sure enough, her mother was singing hymns and dancing with joy. She had placed "Jesus stuff" all over the walls, and her formerly depressed demeanor had completely vanished. Even more convincing to me was the fact that she was dancing without the cane I had always seen her use up until that time. She had stopped her medications and was doing fine! I was shocked and convinced that she had indeed been healed.

At this point, in order to be intellectually honest, I had to be open to following the evidence wherever it led; I was vividly aware that strange things had been going on since that prayer. I flirted with the idea of being at least partially open to the possibility that, if God really did exist, He might be answering my prayer and showing Himself to me after all.

Supernatural events that I had never encountered in my whole life up until that point were suddenly occurring on every side. I also seemed to be running into knowledgeable Christians that I engaged in debate, only to find that they had very reasonable answers to my questions.

I also came across many resources that addressed my doubts, but three journalistic books (written by Lee Strobel) were essential to satisfying my scientific and philosophic thirst for truth in this matter. Strobel, too, was an atheist seeking to expose the Christian faith as fraudulent; rather than approaching random Christians and bullying them with complex questions as I was, Lee had actually sought out knowledgeable Christian theologians, professors, philosophers, and apologists—experienced and expert defenders of the Christian faith. He decided to see what the best minds of the Christian faith had to offer in their argumentation. During that process, Lee became convinced of the truth of Christianity and committed his life to Christ.

The first book I read by Lee was *The Case for a Creator*, which testified to the scientific and philosophical evidences for God and convinced me that the only reasonable conclusion behind the complex design of our universe is an intelligent Mind or God.

The second book was *The Case for Christ*, which made it impossible to come to any other conclusion except that 1) Christ must have been both God and the Messiah as the ancient Hebrew prophecies foretold, and 2) the disciples had truly witnessed His resurrection from the dead.

Lastly, I read *The Case for Faith*, which dealt with the strongest atheistic philosophical arguments against the Christian faith (suffering, death, Hell, etc.) and gave what I thought were satisfactory answers to these tough questions—so much so that, after reading these books, I was totally convinced and reasonably persuaded of the truth of God, Christ, and the Bible's infallibility and divine inspiration.

After reading Strobel's material, I literally had no arguments left. He even addressed additional challenges to the Christian faith that I didn't even know existed! God removed my intellectual doubts, and I felt compelled to follow the evidence where it led me—even if it made me uncomfortable. So I began to believe in Christ—intellectually, at least. I reluctantly proclaimed myself to be a Christian and began attending a church in my area. However, I still continued to comfortably live in an immoral way—but this wouldn't last for very long.

After what I came to refer to as my "weekend of sin," I awoke one morning with powerful feelings of sorrowful regret for the previous drunken mess the night before—and quite frankly, for all the sin of my life. This was another very strange occurrence for me—the sinful habits and practices I had formerly loved began to cause me emotional and spiritual discomfort, pain, distress, and grief. I found myself deeply remorseful to God for what I had done against Him all my life, and it manifested as tearful moments of heartache. I found myself wondering how I could ever live in such a sinful way and yet still honor God. How could I participate in those sins for which the Son of God had received a Roman scourging and a brutal cross? For a week straight, I struggled with the sin that my conscience was now sensitive toward. My soul had begun some sort of process of change—something was happening in me.

The following Friday, I went with Rachel to her church and had the final experience that would send me to my knees. I didn't know those playing the worship on the stage but, during one of the later songs, they stopped. After they stopped, they spoke to the crowd, stating to the effect that someone in this audience has been running from God and now needed to turn himself over to Christ. My mind was now convinced, and my heart was finally struck—here was yet another call from God! It was then that I came to the front of the room and cried out to God on my knees, asking for Him to forgive me of my sins and make me into the person He desired me to be. I vowed that if He would help me to escape the consequences of my sin, that I would dedicate my life to serving Him and telling others about the faith that I once actively tried to destroy.

God began to manifest His presence in my life immediately. Some sins faded away without delay. Excessive swearing was gone without me even working on it—it just effortlessly disappeared. I prayed that God would take away my longstanding addiction to pornography, and it miraculously died the night of that prayer. Other sins lingered on for a while and some I continued to struggle with, but it was true that sins were steadily decreasing their hold on me. I found myself declaring war against them, with new intentions to obey the commands of my God, who had loved me enough to die for my scandalous life.

A growth of wonderful new attributes in me had begun to blossom. I sought out the forgiveness of anyone I could remember having wronged in the past. I stopped those who I had bullied in their tracks on the street to ask for forgiveness. It felt good to humble myself and ask for forgiveness. Patience bloomed, joy budded, and a peace in the soul thrived.

All these things grew and were manifested in me, along with an almost uncontrollable desire to tell the world about Christ and all that He has done, both on the cross and in my life. I didn't know much detail about the Bible at this point or how to communicate the cross in an understandable way yet—but I knew I had to tell the world about Christ, and that He was God, having been resurrected from the dead. His gospel became a part of my life, and His seed bore a fruit-filled vineyard of freedom and love in my soul that continues on this very day.

After these things began to take place, I read later in the Bible that this is what must occur at salvation. The Bible speaks about the Spirit of God (and you can choose your word here) renovating, altering, transforming, developing, or molding you into a new life full of joy, love, faith, and hope in Christ. Paul said in 1 Thessalonians 1:5 that "...our gospel did not come to you in word only, but also in the power and in the Holy Spirit and with full conviction." I learned this truth from the Bible after I had already experienced it in my conversion and encounter with the divine Creator of the universe.

The Testimony of the Experiential Knowledge of God

What I had experienced was on an individual and subjective level, but God had nonetheless manifested Himself and continues to do so whether one chooses to believe me or not. My encounter with God is by no means an isolated event. Similar works like these have been experienced in millions of people—for effectively thousands of years. I am just one of many. My continuous relational experiences of prayer and providential timing are a sort of "spiritual photo album" of God's living presence in my life. It is against these continuous blessed rocks of experience that all doubt against God and Christ were dashed into pieces.

If someone were to ask me, "What would it take to convince you that the God of the Bible doesn't exist?" I would have to admit that no one could convince me. Denying God and His scripture at this point in my life—after all these (and far more) events—would be completely irrational. This would be the equivalent of claiming that my grandpa never existed and that all the pictures of him in the photo albums were faked. Even though he has passed on, I still know that he existed and that the old pictures are an accurate representation of Him, because *I knew him on a personal level.* It is on these experientially-rational grounds that nothing could convince me otherwise. The same can be said about God, both for me and for all true believers in Christ who have encountered Him on the same personal level. We possess an argument of certainty that the atheist could never possess. They will always be uncertain about God because they have never experienced Him, while Christians who have experienced Him can always be certain.

All I can actually demonstrate in this book is that one can reflect upon both natural and personal fingerprints of our Creator, the divinely inspired scripture, the claims of the disciples, the witness of prophecy, and my own experiential testimony—I have nothing else to offer. However, this I can tell you, that anyone who turns from those things that they know to be sinful and believes on Jesus Christ, they too will also experience God for themselves. As a result, you too can be just as convinced through your own experience, as I am, that the God of the Hebrews exists and is actively working today.

Experiences—while they might not be entirely convincing to those looking from the outside—are, for the Christian, a major defeater against many broad forms of skepticism. No one will be able to remove from you what you experientially know to be true.

Conclusion

All people, irrespective of their worldview, have a type of trust—or shall we say faith—in everyday things. When we read information, we generally tend to accept that it is truthful. Why are we willing to so quickly accept such writings as truth? Because those who wrote the articles are generally considered experts, and we trust that the information provided from the experts is somewhat accurate. Unless we are passionate about a particular subject, we won't usually expand our quest for the truthfulness of something beyond a quick glance at the footnotes; we tend to trust it, unless we have reasons to think otherwise.

If it is reasonable to trust that the pharmacist has given you the correct medicine prescribed for you, or to trust a journeyman carpenter to build your home up to quality and the legal standards, then it is just as reasonable for the Christian to trust in the testimony of the apostles and prophets—the same prophets who received accurate prophecies and the same apostles who physically encountered and documented the physically resurrected Christ. They have the best expertise on the person and work of Jesus since they walked with Him for three years and were in possession of their own papers on

Him (i.e. the eyewitness accounts of the Gospels and the letters of the New Testament).

These apostles were disciples (students) walking with their rabbi (teacher), talking with Him, asking Him questions about morals, status, government responsibility, and numerous other things. They did not do this as philosophical thinkers, but as everyday men from different social statuses, speaking to God in the flesh, who knows all things. They came to a unified verdict—that Jesus Christ had indeed fulfilled the messianic prophecies, which unveiled His unique identity. He confirmed this through His claims, miracles, resurrection, and prophecy and now commands all men everywhere to come to Him by faith, turn from their sin in repentance and become baptized into newness of life.

A Visual Faith

Faith is far from being blind. It is defined in the scripture as being "...the assurance of things hoped for, the conviction of things not seen" (Hebrews 11:1). In other words, we deem the Creator of all things to have long ago revealed Himself in the scripture. Though we have not seen God or Christ with our own eyes, we remain convinced of the scripture's authority in certainty. We are assured that the promised declarations of the past, present, and future are reliable and truthfully communicated to us today.

I have faith that my sin is currently forgiven, as the scripture proclaims. I have faith that God has sanctified me in a life that is greatly contrasted since the day I first trusted in Christ. I have faith that, when Christ died long ago, Jesus went purposefully to that cross to purchase my soul, as well as the rest of His elect for eternal life, as the scripture records. These things are trusted by faith; I cannot prove these things in a scientific lab or through scientific reflections—therefore, in these matters, faith is necessary.

In this way, *reason and faith are not in contrast against each other, but rather go hand-in-hand for the Christian*—a reflective harmony, two sides to the same coin. I hold to a similar view as Galileo did, who said, "I do not feel obliged to believe that the same God who endowed us with sense, reason, and intellect had intended for us to forgo their use." God gave us minds so we don't need to forsake the use of them to believe in Him.

It should be obvious by now why millions choose to believe in scripture as their source for truth, and so live according to those commands and principles that God has enclosed within the pages of His Word. The evidence remains open for every eye to see, but will you interpret that evidence through a naturalistic or supernatural framework? Does the evidence suggest blind, naturalistic, materialistic atheism or that a purposeful supernatural God is behind everything?

There is no lack of evidence for God's existence in the natural world. Yet these separate demonstrations of God's glory are a part of the vaster and more convincing whole—a cumulative case. All the evidences, when summed up together, present a rational foundation that the follower of Christ can easily stand upon. Even if you found that some of these separate arguments weren't entirely convincing to you, surely the sum of the presented arguments, taken as a whole, are overwhelmingly in agreement with reasonable inquiry. There is a serious consideration now to be made on your part to either give yourself to Christ today, or seriously and quickly investigate the matter further before it's too late. Christian philosopher Ronald Nash says, when summing up the arguments for God's existence, "Juries in court cases are not required to seek proof beyond all possible doubt, only beyond a *reasonable* doubt."[19]

In this effort, at least, I believe that I have made my case. But make no mistake about it, the stakes in this case are eternally high. Don't make this book a mere intellectual study, but use it to test your heart and seek after Christ. If God does not exist, then it logically follows that the deep answers to life's questions—questions of purpose, morals, order, emotion, justice, instinct, beauty, knowledge, creation, order, cause and effect, and life—are actually unanswerable, unknown, or simply don't exist. Ask yourself—does that sound reasonable? Morality (love, justice, goodness) without a divine source becomes an illusion of the natural world—a byproduct of human evolution where the morality of Hitler and Mother Teresa are on the same moral plane with no higher moral standard to appeal to.

Atheistic, materialistic naturalism fosters a whole host of irrational, contradictory and illogical beliefs that have never been observed—naturalism is a blind faith on steroids. Naturalism supports ideas that are illogical: order arising from chaos, life from non-life, information from randomness, personality from impersonal forces, intelligence from thoughtless substances, and of course, the climax—that all of these things came about when nothingness somehow received energy and exploded into everything we know.

In this way, the naturalistic scientific community is reaching as far as it can in order to maintain a pre-biased rejection of God. H. J. Lipson, a professor of physics from Manchester, writes: "Evolution became in a sense a scientific religion; almost all scientists have accepted it and many are prepared to bend their observations to fit in with it."[20]

Atheism, with its worldview of Darwinian evolution, is an *Alice in Wonderland* story—a fairy tale where up is down and left is right, where nothing is what it seems, and you can believe in six impossible things before breakfast! Dr. T. N. Tahmisian of the atomic energy commission famously stated that "Scientists who go about teaching that evolution is a fact of life are great con-men, and the story they are telling may be the greatest hoax ever. In explaining evolution, we do not have one iota of fact."[21] Why then accept such unscientific conclusions? Let us allow a naturalist scientist to speak for himself and give us—what I suspect to be—the overarching motive. Consider the honesty of a distinguished evolutionary biologist, Richard Lewontin:

> *Our willingness to accept scientific claims that are against common sense is the key to an understanding of the real struggle between science and the supernatural. We take the side of science in spite of the patent absurdity of some of its constructs, in spite of its failure to fulfill many of its extravagant promises of health and life, in spite of the tolerance of the scientific community for unsubstantiated just-so stories, because we have a prior commitment—a commitment to materialism. It is not that the methods and institutions of science somehow compel us to accept a material explanation of the phenomenal world, but, on the contrary, that we are forced by our **a priori** adherence to material causes to create an apparatus of investigation and a set of concepts that produce material explanations, **no matter how counter-intuitive, no matter how mystifying to the uninitiated. Moreover, that materialism is absolute, for we cannot allow a Divine Foot in the door.**[22]*

Many accept naturalistic materialism and reject the reasonable conclusions of theism (specifically Christianity) because it more interferes with personal liberties and sexual "freedoms" rather than sound science. Men would rather set themselves up as a god of their own personal universe rather than surrender submissively before their Creator and His commands. Naturalism and materialism both provide that philosophical escape by allowing one to embrace the divinity of self.

God warns us in 2 Peter 3:3-6 that false teachers will be coming in the last days, attempting to lead others from God and truth:

...scoffers will come in the last days with scoffing, following their own sinful desires. They will say, 'Where is the promise of his coming? For ever since the fathers fell asleep, *all things are continuing as they were from the beginning of creation.*' For they deliberately overlook this fact, that the heavens existed long ago, and the earth was formed out of water and through water by the word of God, and that by means of these the world that then existed was deluged with water and perished.

Science discovers truthful things and makes real predictions only because the world was created and designed with laws that persuade it to act with regularity. We, as the spectators of that reality, are blessed with the cognitive abilities to perceive its wonder and study it from within.

He has revealed His purposeful intentions in His creation and allowed you to be a spectator of it. Our emotional longing after peace, community, acceptance, love, and joy also cannot be not accidental, but purposefully intended by an incredibly intelligent Being for our own good. That Being is not just any generic "god," but the Almighty Yahweh of the Israelites, who has historically revealed Himself through the miraculous works of Christ and His prophetic fulfillment.

I now conclude in asking you, the reader, who is Jesus Christ in the light of history, prophecy, and biblical authority? With this in mind, I now leave you with these closing words from Christ in John 11:25-26:

*I am the resurrection and the life. Whoever **believes** in me, though he die, yet **shall he live**, and everyone who lives and believes in me shall never die. Do you believe this?*

Well... do you believe?

My Final Encouragement

Remember that every material possession that you own, every investment, every plan for the future, and every person in your life will one day fade away as you stand before the God who has created all things. He is the only constant that we will face in a world of disorder, flux, and change. Our most important matter in life, therefore, is that we would make ourselves ready for that approaching Day of Judgment. Pray to God this day and ask for His forgiveness; ask Him to create within you a new heart, that you might know Jesus Christ and experience everlasting peace with God.

The importance of reading the Bible daily and obeying what you read cannot be overemphasized. A few great places to begin with are Genesis 1:1-11, the book of Exodus, the Gospel of John, the book of Romans, and the last four chapters of the book of Revelation. After you've read these passages, you should be able to gain a great elementary, bite-sized overview of the whole Bible. After this, read the Bible through over and over again, learning all God has for you to know.

It is also imperative for your spiritual well-being that you seek a church that will preach directly through the books of the Bible verse by verse as a regular form of worship. Make sure that the preaching and teaching is not just on the comfortable subjects such as love, hope, and faith, but also on the weightier subjects of wrath, repentance, and holiness. You want all of

God's Word, not just motivational speeches on being a good person. You want Christ preached and exalted, since it is in Him our hope is found! Attend this Bible-teaching church regularly for growth in holiness, love, and encouragement, that you might be fixed and grow in the things of God.

Since Christ died for His people, the least His people can do is live for Him. Think upon these things today, for tomorrow may never come. The breath God grants to us is not certain, but our death is.

In Thy Mind

The heavens declare brilliance,
All holds as it should;
Set within Thy Holy Self
All exists, because You could
In a moment it all could fall away,
'Cept that the Lord holdeth on;
Without Thee all shall cease to be
As quickly as it came—gone
Hallelujah, Triune Creator,
The One who breaths life;
Hallelujah to the risen Savior
Who shall bring the end to strife
—JEFF MCCONNELL

Citations

Chapter 2: Observational and Logical Demonstrations of God's Glory

[1] Stephen Hawking, *A Brief History of Time.*

[2] Richard Morris, *The Fate of the Universe*, p.153.

[3] Robert Jastrow, "The Astronomer and God," in *The Intellectuals Speak Out About God*, ed. Roy Abraham Varghese (Chicago: Regenery Gateway, 1984) p. 22. Gog.

[4] Michael Denton, *Evolution: A Theory in Crisis* (Bethesda, Md.: Adler & Adler, 1985), 264.

[5] ICR, *Guide to the Human Body*, Nov 2015, pg. 47.

[6] www.spine-health.com/conditions/spine-anatomy/anatomy-coccyx-tailbone

[7] Sir Fred Hoyle, as quoted by Lee Elliot Major, "Big enough to Bury Darwin". Guardian (UK) education supplement, Thursday August 23, 2001; Fred Hoyle and N. Chandra Wickramasinghe, *Evolution from Space* (London: J.M. Dent & Sons, 1981).

[8] Frances Crick, *Life Itself, Its Origin and Nature*, 1981, pg.88.

[9] P.C.W. Davies, "The Anthropic Principle," in *Particle and Nuclear Physics.*

[10] Wernher von Braun, *Tornado in a Junkyard*, Arlington, pg. 253.

Chapter 3: Relational and Personal Demonstrations of God's Glory

[11] Ronald Nash, *Faith and Reason*, pg. 259, 1988, Zondervan Publishing House.

Chapter 4: Has God Revealed Himself In Any Other Way

[12] The Quran; Translated by Maulana Wahiduddin Khan https://
yassarnalquran.files.wordpress.com/2010/08/quran_maulana_
wahiduddin.pdf

[13] Time, December 18, 1995.

[14] New Answers Book: Over 25 Questions on Creation/Evolution and
the Bible. Pg. 133; June 2012, eighteenth print.

Chapter 5: The Testimony of Jesus Christ

[15] pp. 46 and 53 of The Testimony of the Evangelists, Examined by
the Rules of Evidence Administered in Courts of Justice; 1846.

[16] Sir Lionel Luckhoo, The Question Answered: Did Jesus Rise
from the Dead? Luckhoo Booklets, back page. http://www.
hawaiichristiansonline.com/sir_lionel.html.

[17] Peter W. Stoner, Robert C. Newman, Science Speaks Scientific
Proof of the Accuracy of Prophecy and the Bible; Chapter 3: "The
Christ of Prophecy."

[18] ibid.

Chapter 7: God's Message Part 2: The Good News

[19] Ronald Nash, Faith and Reason, pg. 259, 1988, Zondervan
Publishing House.

[20] "A Physicist Looks at Evolution," Physics Bulletin 31, 1980, pg.138.

[21] T. N. Tahmisian; The Fresno Bee, August 20, 1959, pg.1-B.

[22] Richard Lewontin, "Billions and billions of demons" (review of
The Demon-Haunted World: Science as a Candle in the Dark by
Carl Sagan, The New York Review of Books Copyright, pg. 31, 9
January 1997, by Richard C. Lewontin.

Made in the USA
Columbia, SC
21 September 2020